ROYAL BOROUGH OF GREENWICH

Follow us on twitter @greenwichlibs

Blackheath Libra~
Tel: ~

Please return

05/2021

- 3 JUL 2021

D0513765

Figuring Out the Past

Peter Turchin and Daniel Hoyer

Figuring Out the Past

The 3,495 vital statistics that explain world history

The
Economist BOOKS

Published in 2020 under exclusive licence from *The Economist* by
Profile Books Ltd
29 Cloth Fair
London EC1A 7JQ
www.profilebooks.com

Copyright © The Economist Newspaper Ltd, 2020
Text copyright © Peter Turchin and Daniel Hoyer, 2020

10 9 8 7 6 5 4 3 2 1

A CIP catalogue record for this book is available from the British Library.

ISBN 978 1 78816 192 3
eISBN 978 1 78283 519 6

Design and typesetting by EM&EN
Printed in Great Britain by Bell & Bain Ltd, Glasgow

MIX
Paper from
responsible sources
FSC
www.fsc.org
FSC® C007785

Contents

Rankings

Regional adoption

Maps

Introduction

What was history's biggest empire? What was the tallest building ever constructed before concrete? What was the life expectancy in medieval Byzantium? Where did scientific writing first emerge? What was the bloodiest ever human sacrifice?

We are used to thinking about history in terms of stories: who did what to whom. Yet we understand our own world through data: vast arrays of statistics that reveal the workings of our societies. Why not the past as well? *Figuring Out the Past* turns a quantitative eye on our collective trajectory. Behind the fleeting dramas of individual factions and rulers, it looks for large-scale regularities. It asks how key social and technological innovations spread around the world, and it pinpoints outliers from the general trends.

As historians Jo Guldi and David Armitage wrote in *The History Manifesto*: "in a crisis of short-termism, our world needs somewhere to turn to for information about the relationship between past and future". The book in your hands draws on a vast reservoir of historical data that was collected precisely to serve that need. Seshat: Global History Databank was founded in 2011 with the long-term goal of collecting and indexing as much data about the human past as can be known or credibly estimated. Named after the ancient Egyptian goddess of scribes and record-keeping, Seshat is the work of a large international team of historians, archeologists, anthropologists and other specialists. Inevitably incomplete and constantly being updated, it nevertheless has a strong claim to be the most comprehensive body of information about human history ever assembled in one place. (You can explore it at seshatdatabank.info)

Much as contemporary economic data are used to test theories about the day-to-day evolution of economic systems, Seshat was created to test long-range hypotheses about the rise, workings and fall of societies across the globe. For example, what causes states to develop and spread in the way they have? Why have some societies experienced high levels of growth and well-being while others stagnated? What role have warfare, religion and technology played in the evolution of social institutions? What causes societies to collapse or fracture?

The only way to answer questions like these is to test them against the historical record. Seshat, more than any other resource, collects as much of that record as possible, collated and formatted to make testing practical. The information presented in this book is intended to illustrate some key trends and patterns that emerge when you look at history from Seshat's dizzying vantage point.

A caveat: the figures presented here are only a sample of the data compiled by the Seshat project, which in turn is only a subset of what is known about past societies. All the same, because of the databank's remarkable breadth of scope and through the collaboration of dozens of the world's leading historical experts, the rankings and comparisons that follow are collectively as reliable as could be obtained from any existing resource. They reflect the best, most accurate and most complete information available at the time of writing.

As of 2020, Seshat holds information on over 450 historic societies (identified within the databank itself using the term "polities", to avoid ambiguity). It starts among the first West Asian farming communities in the Neolithic period about 10,000 years ago and ends in the 19th century CE. The Neolithic, in certain regions described as the "Agricultural Revolution", is the time when humans began to settle in one spot and build recognisably distinct communities.

Conversely, the databank stops compiling figures for more modern societies largely because this more recent history is so well known. This book focuses, then, on these lesser-known periods covered by the databank. Nevertheless, data on a handful of 19th- and 20th-century nations are included for comparison among the society profiles that follow. (They are excluded from rankings and comparisons, which are confined to the preindustrial world so as to make room for these less familiar, but nevertheless important, societies to stand out.)

Many of the types of data presented in this book will be familiar to readers of *The Economist*'s annually updated *Pocket World in Figures*. Measures such as society size, populations and life expectancy provide a nearly continuous line from the ancient past to the present day. Others are more exotic, illuminating some of the key traits that distinguished past societies: their agricultural and metallurgic technologies; their governing institutions and provision of public goods; their openness to principles of equality; and so on.

Figuring Out the Past offers sections ranking societies on these items, separated into eras (ancient, medieval, early modern and modern), along with rankings across the eras. It also traces the geographical spread of key technologies and social innovations, from mounted cavalry to coinage, to show where and when some of the most important breakthroughs took place, and how they diffused around the globe. It shows when these crucial innovations arrived in different regions of the world, shining a spotlight on areas often overlooked in global histories, such as sub-Saharan Africa, South America and Polynesia, some of which encountered key technologies for the first time in the ships of colonisers, while others experienced a long history of complex societies and saw indigenous innovations well before the arrival of Europeans, perhaps to the surprise of many readers.

The societies presented here represent those for which the Seshat Databank has well-curated data. As many of these may be unfamiliar to readers, the book contains detailed society profiles which offer a close look at their make-up with respect to a common set of key indicators, along with short introductions highlighting useful information about each.

Taken together, the figures and profiles collected here show how far we have come as a species over the past 10,000 years: from our origins in roving hunter-gatherer bands, to the first settled villages and small chiefdoms, to archaic states ruled by "god-kings" wielding nearly unlimited authority, to modern nation-states populated by hundreds of millions of people powered by ever-evolving technologies.

More than this, however, these figures show how much we all have in common, both with our ancestors and with each other. We all share the need to organise and maintain social cohesion among large and diverse populations. We all have to innovate to survive in changing physical and social environments, to bolster ourselves against the vicissitudes of natural disasters and to interact with neighbours (who may not have peaceful intentions). There is, moreover, a deep continuity in our symbolic lives. We all build glorious monuments to our own ingenuity and creativity. We all seem compelled to develop rituals to create a shared sense of identity. We all have ideals that we strive to live up to.

These concerns have occupied our species at least since before we first started to settle in agrarian villages. One truth that Seshat demonstrates is that, along with many unique milestones that were reached at different places and times, there are plenty of immutable patterns in our shared history. The more things change, the more they stay the same. And nothing makes this fact clearer than a close look at the data.

Acknowledgements

This work would not have been completed without the tireless work and dedication of the Seshat research team. We would like to single out especially Enrico Cioni, Jill Levine, Jenny Reddish, Edward Turner, Sal Wiltshire and Gregory Youmans, who compiled and checked much of the data found in this volume. We gratefully acknowledge the invaluable assistance we receive from our collaborators, who ensure that Seshat holds the most comprehensive, up-to-date information possible. In particular, we thank the following for reviewing portions of this volume (though any remaining mistakes are entirely our own): Mark Altaweel, Abel Alves, John Baines, Jim Bennett, David Carballo, Metin Cosgel, Alan Covey, Gary Feinman, Patrick Kirch, Andrey Korotayev, Nikolay Kradin, John Miksic, Ruth Mostern, Alessio Palmisano, Peter Peregrine, Johannes Preiser-Kapeller and Katrinka Reinhart. Please see the Seshat website (seshatdatabank.info) for a full list of private donors, partners, experts and consultants, along with their respective areas of expertise.

Explanation of terms

Life expectancy from birth – the average age to which people in a society lived, including the often large numbers who died in infancy. Other calculations (such as "average age at death") often leave out those who died before the age of 5, which results in a higher figure.

Irrigation & drinking water, Health care, Alimentary support, Famine relief – refer to welfare run and financed by the state, unless noted otherwise.

Long walls – permanent fortifications used to protect a large territory rather than a single settlement.

Society
profiles

Ancient: 3000 BCE to 500 CE

Egypt: Old Kingdom

In the centuries before 3000 BCE, one of the world's earliest states (rivalled only by Mesopotamian societies) emerged in the Nile Valley in what is today Egypt. During the Old Kingdom, the period of Egyptian history from around 2650 to 2150 BCE, towering pyramids were built from stone to serve as tombs for divine kings and their queens. The largest, the Great Pyramid at Giza, stood 147 m high and was originally faced with dazzlingly white smooth-dressed limestone.

General
Duration 2650–2150 BCE
Language Ancient Egyptian (Afro-Asiatic)
Preceded by Early Dynastic period Egypt
Succeeded by Period of the Regions or First Intermediate period

Territory
Total area (km²) 75,000–350,000. Difficult to provide precise estimates because it is unclear how much of desert territory surrounding the Nile valley was state controlled.

People
Population 1–1.5m
Largest city No data (Memphis)
Standing army 20,000. State-maintained officer class; expeditions

sourced using conscription and some non-Egyptian military personnel.

Social scale

Settlement hierarchy 1. Capital city; 2. Regional centres; 3. Minor centres; 4. Small settlements; 5. Hamlets.

Administrative hierarchy 1. King (Pharaoh); 2. Vizier; 3. Overseers; 4. Controllers; 5. Inspectors; 6. Under-supervisors; 7. Scribes.

Institutions

Legal code Probably absent. There were property laws and formal written legal instruments, though no evidence for a fully articulated legal code.

Bureaucracy Professional. Several major administrative departments, eg treasury, granaries and other public works.

Religious validation of rule King was thought to be under the patronage of the gods, at times seen as a living god himself; he preserved *maat* (order, justice, righteousness) on the gods' behalf and for the good of the Egyptian people.

Property rights Private property existed.

Price controls Absent

Banking regulations Absent

Economy

Taxation Taxes levied primarily on land and its products.

Coinage Absent

Credit Probably present. Debt structures suggest availability of credit.

Agricultural practices

Main crops Emmer wheat and barley

Irrigation Present, though agriculture mainly relied on inundation from the annual flooding of the Nile.

Fertilising Probably present, though direct evidence is sparse.

Cropping system Nutrient replacement of soil with annual flooding

Metallurgy

Base metal Evidence for copper metallurgy from c. 3000 BCE

Military equipment

Handheld weapons Battle axes, copper-tipped spears, daggers, war clubs and maces.

Armour Wooden parrying sticks and wooden shields covered in cowhide.

Projectiles Returning throw sticks, sling shots, bows and arrows

Incendiaries Inferred absent

Long walls Evidence of some city walls

Well-being

Life expectancy 20–30 years from birth

Average adult stature 169 cm (male); 160 cm (female)

Irrigation & drinking water Irrigation canals and flood control measures present by 2500 BC; desert wells dating long before, possibly from prehistoric period.

Health care Ritual practitioners and physicians (*swnw*) used both material methods, such as surgery and drugs, and supernatural methods such as incantations and magical objects.

Alimentary support Moral duty of the wealthy to give aid to the poor.

Famine relief King and local high officials obliged to distribute grain from granaries in event of food shortage.

(In)equalities

Social mobility Unclear, though there are indications of a largely hereditary elite. Increase in wealth of tombs of lower officials towards the end of this period suggests an increase in mobility.

Occupational mobility Rise in the number of craftspeople towards

6

the end of this period suggests an increase in occupational mobility, or reduction in social inequality.

Gender equality Women could be priests or hold high positions in certain professions, often related to ritual activity; daughters could inherit as much as sons; non-royal marriage was monogamous.

Slavery Enslaved people were few in number, especially compared with other ancient societies across Afro-Eurasia.

Human sacrifice Unclear. Probably absent, but possible that war captives were sacrificed.

Religion

Majority religious practice Ancient Egyptian religion. State religion centring around the king, considered a divine ruler, dependent on and answerable to the gods; there was great diversity in ritual practice in the wider population, centred around a large canon of supernatural beings.

Iraq: Akkadians

The Akkadian Empire (c. 2300–2100 BCE) was founded through the military conquests of Sargon of Akkad, who unified the various cities of Mesopotamia under one monarchy to create the first true empire in human history. It encompassed much of modern-day Iraq and Syria, but the location of the city of Akkad itself remains unknown. Akkadian kings governed with the aid of strongly fortified settlements, a large standing army and written record-keeping using the cuneiform script.

General
Duration 2270–2083 BCE
Languages Akkadian and Sumerian
Preceded by Lagash dynasty
Succeeded by Gutian dynasty

Territory
Total area (km²) 1.1m in 2200 BCE

People
Population >210,000. Estimates for total urban population of Akkadian Empire in 2200 BCE.
Largest city 20,000–40,000 (possibly Adab)
Standing army 5,400: King Sargon claimed his army had a backbone of 5,400 men.

Social scale
Settlement hierarchy 1. Capital (Agade); 2. Major administrative

centres; 3. Lesser centres specialised in revenue collection;
4. Towns; 5. Villages.
Administrative hierarchy 1. King; 2. Civil administrator (*shaperum*);
3. Land registrar; 4. Governors (*ensis*); 5. Scribes and surveyors.

Institutions

Legal code Mixed. Unknown whether Akkad had a formal legal code,
but a complex legal system is attested by documents that record
litigation.

Bureaucracy Professional. Scribes, registrars, surveyors, inspectors,
tax assessors supervised by civil administrator (*shaperum*).

Religious validation of rule King seen as preserving order on behalf of
the gods.

Property rights Private ownership of land recognised throughout the
third millennium in the region.

Price controls Some evidence for price controls by kings to prevent
price inflation by producers that hurt the poor.

Banking regulations Probably absent

Economy

Taxation Taxes on barley yields, livestock, irrigated water use,
property inheritance in urban areas, grazing rights and boat
transport.

Coinage Absent. Uncoined silver used as money.

Credit Merchants provided loans. Farm workers earned one shekel of
silver a month.

Agricultural practices

Main crops Wheat and barley
Irrigation Present
Fertilising Probably present in Mesopotamian regions
Cropping system Fallowing, two-field rotation and nitrogen-fixing
crops.

Metallurgy
Base metal Bronze

Military equipment
Handheld weapons War clubs, maces, battle axes, daggers and spears; swords probably present but not in common use on the battlefield.

Armour Helmets of felt, leather or copper; tough fabric or leather sash may have covered the chest; reference to shields in texts.

Projectiles Javelins, slings, throw-sticks, bows and arrows

Incendiaries No evidence

Long walls No evidence

Well-being
Life expectancy No data

Average adult stature No data

Irrigation & drinking water Mixed. Extensive irrigation system in "breadbasket" region (Sumer), smaller local wells in towns but no evidence for large-scale drinking water supply system.

Health care Evidence for sanitation systems such as underground sewage in elite households. Physicians known in Mesopotamia since 2500 BCE; texts suggest existence of dentists in Akkadian period.

Alimentary support Unclear. No concrete evidence, but ideological expectation for rulers to be charitable.

Famine relief Unclear. No concrete evidence, but state ran bakeries to provide bread and beer to soldiers and workers.

(In)equalities
Social mobility Expanding opportunities, in military and mercantile fields especially.

Occupational mobility Expanding opportunities, in military and mercantile fields especially.

Gender equality Women could possess their own property and
transact on their own behalf; marriage was usually monogamous
(except among elites); engagement terms had legal standing
enforceable in the courts.

Slavery Debt and chattel slavery

Human sacrifice Sacrifices performed at the beginning of the
construction of certain important buildings, though somewhat
rare and on a small scale.

Religion

Majority religious practice Mesopotamian religion. Akkadians prayed
to a pantheon of gods (*ana*) as well as to spirits (*zi*) of the sky,
earth and underworld who could help them. Priests sought
supernatural intervention through ritual hymns and spells and
attempted to divine the future. The Akkadian ruling family
spread an official cult through priests attached to temples. The
king's most important responsibility was as the gods' order-
bringer.

China: Erlitou culture

The Erlitou culture (c. 1900–1500 BCE) was a Bronze Age culture of the Middle Yellow River Valley in modern-day China. Centred on the eponymous site, southeast of the modern city of Luoyang, it is known for its monumental elite earthen architecture, bronze-casting technology and high-quality pottery and jade artefacts. The culture spread widely through the Middle Yellow River Valley, but the level of political authority that the elites at the site of Erlitou exercised over the region remains uncertain. Some historians believe that Erlitou itself was one of the seats of the first dynasty of China, the Xia.

General

Duration 1900–1500 BCE
Language Archaic Chinese (Sino-Tibetan)
Preceded by Longshan culture
Succeeded by Erligang culture or Early Shang dynasty

Territory

Total area (km²) 10,000–20,000. Estimate based on extent of material culture finds.

People

Population Unclear. Perhaps 50,000–80,000 throughout Erlitou cultural sphere.
Largest city 18,000–30,000 (Erlitou). Estimate based on archaeological remains.
Standing army No data

Social scale

Settlement hierarchy 1. Erlitou; 2. Large settlements; 3. Medium-size settlements; 4. Small settlements.

Administrative hierarchy 1. Ruler or chief priest; 2. Administrator; 3. Scribe.

Institutions

Legal code No data

Bureaucracy No data. A "proto-bureaucracy" may well have existed but, overall, the evidence is thin.

Religious validation of rule No data

Property rights No data

Price controls Probably absent

Banking regulations No data

Economy

Taxation No data

Coinage Absent

Credit No data

Agricultural practices

Main crops Millet. Wheat, tubers and rice known as well.

Irrigation Present

Fertilising Absent

Cropping system Swidden farming and two-field rotation evidenced.

Metallurgy

Base metal Bronze

Military equipment

Handheld weapons Adzes, knives, axes, dagger-axes and clubs

Armour No evidence

Projectiles Bows and throwing spears

Incendiaries No evidence

Long walls No evidence

Well-being

Life expectancy 23–35 average age at death (total population). Estimate from sparse archaeological remains.

Average adult stature 166 cm (male); 157 cm (female)

Irrigation & drinking water No data

Health care No data

Alimentary support No data

Famine relief No data

(In)equalities

Social mobility Hereditary elite

Occupational mobility Absent

Gender equality Unclear. Some evidence of patriarchal social structure, such as different burial practices.

Slavery Unclear. Some argue that this was the earliest society in China practising slavery, though others claim there is no concrete evidence of a servile population.

Human sacrifice Evidence for sacrificial remains at the Erlitou site itself as well as nearby sites. For example, children bound and buried in pits and under housing foundations at the Erligang site of Yanshi Shangcheng.

Religion

Majority religious practice Chinese folk religion. Involved ancestor worship and animal bone divination.

Turkey: Hittite Empire

The Hittite Empire (or Hittite New Kingdom) flourished in the Late Bronze Age, c. 1400–1180 BCE. At its height in the mid-14th century, the Hittite king controlled up to 400,000 km² of land encompassing much of what is today Turkey along with parts of Syria, Israel–Palestine and Iraq. Building on earlier developments to the south in Mesopotamia, Hittite rule was strong, centralised and bureaucratic. However, shortly after 1200 BCE the empire fell apart rapidly amid the widespread conflict and settlement destruction during the Late Bronze Age crisis, the causes of which are still hotly debated.

General
Duration 1400–1180 BCE
Language Nesite (Indo-European)
Preceded by Hatti – Old kingdom
Succeeded by Neo-Hittite kingdoms

Territory
Total area (km²) 250,000–350,000 in 1300 BCE; 300,000–400,000 in 1200 BCE.

People
Population 1.3m–2m
Largest city 15,000–20,000 (Hattusa)
Standing army 30,000

Social scale
Settlement hierarchy 1. Capital (Hattusa); 2. Large settlements; 3. Villages; 4. Farmsteads.

Egypt: New Kingdom

The Egyptian New Kingdom, c. 1550–1070 BCE, represents what many consider to be the height of Egyptian civilisation. It was during this period that rulers such as Ahmose I, Thutmose III and Ramesses II mounted military campaigns into Nubia (modern Sudan) to the south and the Levant to the northeast, expanding the sphere of Egyptian control to its greatest extent. The New Kingdom also saw a florescence of monumental architecture, art and literature as well as a short-lived quasi-monotheistic religious revolution under the pharaoh Akhenaten.

General
Duration 1550–1070 BCE
Language Late Egyptian (Afro-Asiatic)
Preceded by Thebes-Hyksos period
Succeeded by Thebes-Libyan dynasties

Territory
Total area (km²) 650,000 in 1500 BCE; 1m in 1400 BCE; 900,000 in 1300 BCE; 750,000 in 1200 BCE; 560,000 in 1100 BCE. Figures include wide estimates of controlled desert territory around the Nile Valley.

People
Population 3m–7m
Largest city 50,000–60,000 (Thebes and Memphis) in 1500 BCE; 60,000–80,000 (Thebes) in 1400–1300 BCE; 160,000 (Per-Ramesses) in 1200 BCE; 100,000–120,000 (Per-Ramesses) in 1100 BCE.

Administrative hierarchy 1. King; 2. Chief of the Scribes; 3. Scribe of the Wooden Tablets; 4. Lesser scribes and officials; 5. Scribal assistants.

Institutions
Legal code Present
Bureaucracy Professional
Religious validation of rule King and queen were high priest and priestess of the official cult.
Property rights Many laws dealing with theft or damage to property.
Price controls No data
Banking regulations No data

Economy
Taxation Taxes on land and agriculture; farmers on royal land could pay with their labour on state projects.
Coinage Absent
Credit Probably present

Agricultural practices
Main crop Wheat
Irrigation Present
Fertilising Present
Cropping system Short-fallowing

Metallurgy
Base metals Bronze was present; iron appeared towards the end of the period.

Military equipment
Handheld weapons Spears, daggers, axes and swords
Armour Bronze (and possibly iron) scale armour, chain mail, bronze helmets, shields and limb protection.

Projectiles Composite bows and javelins

Incendiaries No evidence

Long walls No evidence

Well-being

Life expectancy No data

Average adult stature No data

Irrigation & drinking water District governors responsible for maintaining irrigation canals; cisterns dug to collect rainwater.

Health care Unclear. Ideological expectation for ruler to be charitable, but no evidence for legal mechanisms for state provision of welfare services.

Alimentary support Unclear. Ideological expectation for ruler to be charitable, but no evidence for legal mechanisms for state provision of welfare services.

Famine relief Ideological expectation for ruler to be charitable, and there is literary evidence that kings organised grain imports from Egypt during times of shortage.

(In)equalities

Social mobility Hereditary elite. Marriage allowed for some mobility, and wealthy tradespeople were known to have gained higher status.

Occupational mobility Possibly medium/high with regards to craft-making; limited elsewhere.

Gender equality Little known about commoner women, but elite women could attain considerable power, particularly within religious institutions.

Slavery Debtors and war captives were enslaved; chattel slavery existed as well.

Human sacrifice Unclear. Some evidence for the performance of human sacrifice in connection with military engagements.

Religion

Majority religious practice Hittite religion. Hittites believed a multitude of gods inhabited the Heavens, Earth and Underworld.

Standing army 20,000 in 1570–1301 BCE; 25,000–50,000 in 1300–1250 BCE; 10,000–20,000 in 1249–1070 BCE.

Social scale
Settlement hierarchy 1. Capital; 2. Regional centres; 3. Medium-sized settlements; 4. Small settlements; 5. Hamlets.

Administrative hierarchy 1. King (Pharaoh); 2. Vizier; 3. Overseers; 4. Lower-level officials; 5. Scribes.

Institutions
Legal code Possibly present. There appears to have been a legal system with a hierarchy of courts, but it is unclear if there was any formalised legal code.

Bureaucracy Several major administrative departments, eg treasury, granaries and other public works, overseen by vizier.

Religious validation of rule Pharaoh notionally descended from the gods; maintained *maat* (order, justice and righteousness) on their behalf.

Property rights Private property existed.

Price controls Absent

Banking regulations Absent

Economy
Taxation Taxes on land, property, production, trade

Coinage Absent

Credit Unclear. Presence of debt suggests credit structures probably present.

Agricultural practices
Main crops Emmer wheat and barley

Irrigation Present

Fertilising Present

Cropping system Nutrient replacement of soil with annual flooding

Metallurgy
Base metals Copper, bronze and perhaps iron towards the end of the
period

Military equipment
Handheld weapons Battle axes, daggers, spears, long swords and
sickle-shaped swords (*kopesh*).
Armour Shields, cloth padding for limb protection, bronze helmets
and scale armour.
Projectiles Javelins, slings, stave and composite bows
Incendiaries Absent
Long walls City walls known.

Well-being
Life expectancy 20–30 years from birth
Average adult stature 161 cm (male); 156 cm (female)
Irrigation & drinking water State irrigated new areas and developed
canal network; wells widespread.
Health care Ritual practitioners and physicians (*swnw*) used both
material methods, such as surgery and drugs, and supernatural
methods such as incantations and magical objects.
Alimentary support Moral duty for wealthy to give aid to the poor.
Famine relief Pharaohs and local high officials obliged to distribute
grain from granaries in event of food shortage.

(In)equalities
Social mobility Unclear, though there are indications of a largely
hereditary elite.
Occupational mobility Unclear; evidence that many elite men were
engaged in several different professions.
Gender equality Women could own property and enter contracts and
had the same legal rights as men; however, they were barred
from most priestly roles and all professions.

Slavery Some chattel slavery was practised, but not widespread.

Human sacrifice Perhaps foreign enemies were sacrificed on
occasion, but unclear if this was sacrifice or execution.

Religion

Majority religious practice Ancient Egyptian religion. This was a
polytheistic system with Amun-Ra as supreme god; the pharaoh
Akhenaten attempted to introduce a quasi-monotheistic cult of
the sun god Ra in the 14th century, but it did not outlast him.
There was great diversity in ritual practice in the wider
population, centred around a large canon of supernatural beings.

Mexico: Monte Albán, early classic period

The period between c. 200 and 700 CE is generally regarded as a golden age of the Zapotec state in what is now southern Mexico. At their hilltop capital, Monte Albán, the Zapotecs built monumental architecture such as temples, ball courts and paved plazas. These buildings dominate what can be seen at the ruins of the site today. The elites at Monte Albán controlled all of the Oaxaca Valley and exerted some sort of control over adjacent regions, such as the Cuicatlán Cañada and Valley of Ejutla. They engaged in diplomatic relations with the larger state capital of neighbouring Teotihuacán, located 370 km to the north, outside today's Mexico City. Following the collapse of the Teotihuacán state c. 550 CE, Zapotec political organisation became more fragmented, with local elites co-opting the authority once centralised at Monte Albán.

General
Duration 200–700 CE
Language Zapotec (Oto-Manguean)
Preceded by Monte Albán, Late Pre-classic
Succeeded by Monte Albán, Late Classic

Territory
Total area (km²) 20,000 in 200 CE; 3,000 in 700 CE

People
Population 75,000–150,000
Largest city 15,000–30,000 (Monte Albán)
Standing army No data

Social scale

Settlement hierarchy 1. Primary centres (eg Monte Albán);
2. Secondary centres (eg Jalieza); 3. Tertiary centres; 4. Small
settlements.

Administrative hierarchy 1. Capital centre (Monte Albán); 2. Regional
administrative centres; 3. Local administrative centres. This
structure was present from roughly 100 BCE until 500 CE.

Institutions

Legal code No data

Bureaucracy No data

Religious validation of rule Iconography suggests that rulers and
other elites presented themselves as conduits to the realm of the
gods, intermediaries between humans and deities.

Property rights No data

Price controls No data

Banking regulations No data

Economy

Taxation No definitive evidence, but probably some tax system
organised through Monte Albán.

Coinage Absent

Credit No data

Agricultural practices

Main crop Maize

Irrigation Small-scale irrigation, such as check-dams and small
canals.

Fertilising Present

Cropping system One- or two-field rotation depending on access to
water.

Metallurgy

Base metals Absent

Military equipment

Handheld weapons Obsidian knives and wooden clubs; thrusting spears used for hunting could also have been used in warfare.

Armour No definitive evidence for armour; probably made out of perishable materials (eg fabric).

Projectiles *Atlatls*, which flung spear-like darts; slings for projecting stone and ceramic slingshot.

Incendiaries No evidence

Long walls Monte Albán was fortified with long, low walls.

Well-being

Life expectancy No data

Average adult stature 160 cm (male); 147 cm (female)

Irrigation & drinking water Small-scale irrigation likely; no evidence for large state-maintained canal networks or similar, with the possible exception of a reservoir in Monte Albán itself.

Health care No data

Alimentary support No data

Famine relief No data

(In)equalities

Social mobility Hereditary elite, manifest largely in scale and opulence of architecture in elite residences.

Occupational mobility Hierarchical society

Gender equality Royal descent traced through male line, but some examples of powerful female rulers (depicted in male garb).

Slavery No data

Human sacrifice Iconography suggests human sacrifice took place in connection with military campaigns.

Religion

Majority religious practice Monte Albán religion. Besides royal
   ancestors, many gods have been identified, often associated with
   natural elements or entities (eg maize, saurian, snakes, jaguars).

Greece: Alexander the Great's Empire

More than 2,000 years after his birth, Alexander III of Macedon remains one of history's most famous figures. In 336 BCE, when he inherited the throne from his father Philip, Macedonia was a kingdom on the northern fringes of the Greek world, but over his 13-year reign he conquered vast tracts of land, building an empire stretching from Egypt to India (some 4.5 million km^2 of territory). Though his generals carved the empire into smaller kingdoms after his death, Alexander's campaigns had a lasting effect on the character of urbanism and government in the conquered regions, leading to the establishment of Greek-style cities as far east as Afghanistan.

General
Duration 336–294 BCE
Language Ancient Greek (Indo-European)
Preceded by Kingdom of Macedonia
Succeeded by Hellenistic kingdoms

Territory
Total area (km^2) 10,000 in 359 BCE; 5.2m in 320 BCE; 4.4m in 300 BCE

People
Population 20–50m
Largest city 200,000–400,000 (Babylon)
Standing army 40,000–45,000 in Alexander's Macedonian forces

Social scale
Settlement hierarchy 1. Capital (Babylon); 2. Satrapy capitals;
    3. Towns; 4. Villages; 5. Hamlets.

Egypt: New Kingdom

The Egyptian New Kingdom, c. 1550–1070 BCE, represents what many consider to be the height of Egyptian civilisation. It was during this period that rulers such as Ahmose I, Thutmose III and Ramesses II mounted military campaigns into Nubia (modern Sudan) to the south and the Levant to the northeast, expanding the sphere of Egyptian control to its greatest extent. The New Kingdom also saw a florescence of monumental architecture, art and literature as well as a short-lived quasi-monotheistic religious revolution under the pharaoh Akhenaten.

General
Duration 1550–1070 BCE
Language Late Egyptian (Afro-Asiatic)
Preceded by Thebes-Hyksos period
Succeeded by Thebes-Libyan dynasties

Territory
Total area (km²) 650,000 in 1500 BCE; 1m in 1400 BCE; 900,000 in 1300 BCE; 750,000 in 1200 BCE; 560,000 in 1100 BCE. Figures include wide estimates of controlled desert territory around the Nile Valley.

People
Population 3m–7m
Largest city 50,000–60,000 (Thebes and Memphis) in 1500 BCE; 60,000–80,000 (Thebes) in 1400–1300 BCE; 160,000 (Per-Ramesses) in 1200 BCE; 100,000–120,000 (Per-Ramesses) in 1100 BCE.

Human sacrifice Unclear. Some evidence for the performance of
human sacrifice in connection with military engagements.

Religion
Majority religious practice Hittite religion. Hittites believed a
multitude of gods inhabited the Heavens, Earth and Underworld.

Projectiles Composite bows and javelins

Incendiaries No evidence

Long walls No evidence

Well-being

Life expectancy No data

Average adult stature No data

Irrigation & drinking water District governors responsible for
maintaining irrigation canals; cisterns dug to collect
rainwater.

Health care Unclear. Ideological expectation for ruler to be
charitable, but no evidence for legal mechanisms for state
provision of welfare services.

Alimentary support Unclear. Ideological expectation for ruler to
be charitable, but no evidence for legal mechanisms for state
provision of welfare services.

Famine relief Ideological expectation for ruler to be charitable,
and there is literary evidence that kings organised grain imports
from Egypt during times of shortage.

(In)equalities

Social mobility Hereditary elite. Marriage allowed for some mobility,
and wealthy tradespeople were known to have gained higher
status.

Occupational mobility Possibly medium/high with regards to
craft-making; limited elsewhere.

Gender equality Little known about commoner women, but elite
women could attain considerable power, particularly within
religious institutions.

Slavery Debtors and war captives were enslaved; chattel slavery
existed as well.

Administrative hierarchy 1. King; 2. Chief of the Scribes; 3. Scribe of the Wooden Tablets; 4. Lesser scribes and officials; 5. Scribal assistants.

Institutions

Legal code Present

Bureaucracy Professional

Religious validation of rule King and queen were high priest and priestess of the official cult.

Property rights Many laws dealing with theft or damage to property.

Price controls No data

Banking regulations No data

Economy

Taxation Taxes on land and agriculture; farmers on royal land could pay with their labour on state projects.

Coinage Absent

Credit Probably present

Agricultural practices

Main crop Wheat

Irrigation Present

Fertilising Present

Cropping system Short-fallowing

Metallurgy

Base metals Bronze was present; iron appeared towards the end of the period.

Military equipment

Handheld weapons Spears, daggers, axes and swords

Armour Bronze (and possibly iron) scale armour, chain mail, bronze helmets, shields and limb protection.

Administrative hierarchy 1. Emperor / Great King; 2. Military generals (*diadochi*); 3. Court advisors; 4.Provincial governors (*satraps* or *strategoi*); 5. Local rulers; 6. Village leaders.

Institutions

Legal code Present

Bureaucracy Bureaucratic systems of conquered peoples left in place.

Religious validation of rule Alexander the Great and his successors were considered gods by most subjects, particularly in Persian regions, though probably not in Aegean or Macedonian regions.

Property rights Mixed. The Emperor owned all land he conquered ("spear-won land") but could then choose to give it to his generals, or to free cities, or permit its use by his subjects in exchange for tax payments.

Price controls Absent

Banking regulations Absent

Economy

Taxation Harbour dues, land and sales taxes are all known, as is a kind of tax that involved some sort of obligation to community service.

Coinage Present

Credit Attested in Aegean and Macedonian regions. In Ancient Greek economy, bankers offered services such as money-changing and testing, formal loan provision, safe-keeping and escrow, and investment opportunities.

Agricultural practices

Main crops Wheat; olives, grapes, barley and other crops grown in various parts of the Empire.

Irrigation Present in many parts of the vast Empire

Fertilising Present in many parts of the vast Empire

Cropping system Crop rotation practised throughout Aegean, Macedonian and Persian heartlands.

Metallurgy
Base metals Bronze, iron and steel

Military equipment
Handheld weapons *Sarissas* (a kind of thrusting spear), swords and daggers.
Armour Stomach band (*kotthybos*), helmets, shields and greaves; breastplates for officers only.
Projectiles Slings, simple bows, composite bows and crossbows
Incendiaries No evidence
Long walls No evidence

Well-being
Life expectancy No data
Average adult stature 155 cm (male)
Irrigation & drinking water Pre-existing irrigation systems left in place.
Health care No data
Alimentary support Unclear. Mediterranean culture valued prosocial spending on public goods generally, but it is unclear how much this was adopted.
Famine relief Mediterranean culture valued prosocial spending on public goods generally, but it is unclear how much this was adopted.

(In)equalities
Social mobility For men, there was the opportunity to climb military ranks.
Occupational mobility For men, there was the opportunity to climb military ranks.

Gender equality Dominant Greek ideology confined women to the domestic sphere in Aegean and Macedonian regions; elite women in Persian regions had more legal and social rights.

Slavery Common fate of war captives.

Human sacrifice Probably absent

Religion

Majority religious practices Ancient Greek religion. As a result of conquests, Near Eastern deities were added to the pantheon, eg, Isis and Sarapis from Egypt. Also Zoroastrianism; Ancient Egyptian religion; Judaism.

India: Mauryan Empire

The Mauryan Empire, c. 324–187 BCE, was founded when Chandra-gupta Maurya overthrew the ruler of the kingdom of Magadha in the central Ganges plain. With the aid of thousands of war elephants, he conquered a large swathe of land to the west, including territories where Alexander the Great had installed Macedonian *satraps* (governors). At the height of Mauryan power under Ashoka the Great, the empire encompassed most of the subcontinent and extended into eastern Iran. Today, however, Ashoka is most famous for renouncing violence and embracing Buddhism to atone for his bloody conquest of the Kalinga kingdom.

General
Duration 324–187 BCE
Languages Prakrit (Indo-European); Sanskrit (Indo-European). Both used in administration.
Preceded by Nanda Empire
Succeeded by Shunga Empire

Territory
Total area (km²) 4m

People
Population 20m–100m. Wide range of estimates, but larger ones tend to derive from uncritical interpretations of ancient records.
Largest city 50,000–300,000 (Pataliputra)
Standing army 300,000–600,000

Social scale

Settlement hierarchy 1. Capital (Pataliputra); 2. Secondary centres;
   3. Towns; 4. Villages.

Administrative hierarchy 1. King; 2. Top officials (*mantriparishad*);
   3. State administrators; 4. Regional division commissioners
   (*pradeshtris*); 5. State and regional ministers; 6. District officials;
   7. Village officials (*gopas* and *gramikas*).

Institutions

Legal code Present

Bureaucracy Professional. Complex administrative system consisting
   of a council of officials (*mantriparishad*) and departments led by
   professional officials (*adhyakshas*).

Religious validation of rule Right to rule based on heredity and
   military power, though kings also claimed to be "beloved by
   gods".

Property rights Land was theoretically the property of the king but
   practically the property of those who cultivated it.

Price controls Activities of traders and guilds controlled by the state.

Banking regulations Absent

Economy

Taxation Taxes on trade, land and income (eg a sex worker was taxed
   two-days' pay every month).

Coinage Punch-marked silver-copper alloy coin (*masakas*) was
   widespread throughout the empire but came into use before
   Mauryan rule.

Credit Guilds, merchants and the state treasury provided banking
   services.

Agricultural practices

Main crops Millet, rice, barley, wheat and pulses

Irrigation Present

Fertilising Probably absent

Cropping system Nitrogen-fixing crops

Metallurgy

Base metals Bronze, iron and steel

Military equipment

Handheld weapons Clubs, iron maces, battle axes, dagger-axes, lances, spears, swords, daggers and *tomaras* (long spears used by elephant troops).

Armour Infantry carried shields; elite troops had metal breastplates, chain mail, scale, laminar and plate armour, limb protection; no helmets.

Projectiles Javelins, slings, bamboo bows that fired cane arrows, composite bows (*sarngas*).

Incendiaries Used in sieges

Long walls No evidence. Some cities were protected by moats and stone walls.

Well-being

Life expectancy No data

Average adult stature No data

Irrigation & drinking water State built and maintained reservoirs, tanks, canals, wells and storehouses for drinking water.

Health care Inscriptions suggest Mauryan hospitals were state-funded institutions for birth-giving, medical operations and the production and distribution of medicines.

Alimentary support Probably present. According to the treatise on governance, Kautilya's *Arthashastra*, the king should assist the vulnerable.

Famine relief According to the treatise on governance, Kautilya's *Arthashastra*, the king should assist the vulnerable.

(In)equalities

Social mobility Caste system

Occupational mobility Caste system

Gender equality Male-dominated society; to different extents, Buddhism, Jainism and Brahmanism fostered inequality between sexes.

Slavery Not challenged by Buddhist ideals despite its egalitarian ethics.

Human sacrifice Unclear. Forbidden by Buddhism, but non-Buddhists may have practised some form of human sacrifice.

Religion

Majority religious practices Mahayana Buddhism; Jainism; Brahmanism.

Mali: Jenné-jenno

Located along the Middle Niger river, Jenné-jenno is one of the
oldest known cities in sub-Saharan Africa. It was occupied between
c. 250 BCE and 1400 CE and survives as a large "tell": a mound made
up of layers of debris. Archaeological work at several urban clusters
in the region has shown that cities and complex societies have a
long history in West Africa. However, they may have been organised along different lines from early civilisations elsewhere: despite
evidence of sophisticated iron metallurgy, craft specialisation and
high population densities, there is no sign of any ruling elite or
centralised administration.

General
Duration 400–900 CE
Languages Unclear. Region was part of the Mande-speaking cultural
sphere, but unclear what early inhabitants of Jenné-jenno spoke.
Preceded by Jenné-jenno (early phases)
Succeeded by Wagadu kingdom

Territory
Total area (km²) 1,100

People
Population 10,000–26,000
Largest city 7,000 (Jenné-jenno)
Standing army No data. No clear evidence for warfare during this
period.

Social scale

Settlement hierarchy 1. Large centres (eg Jenné-jenno); 2. Medium-sized settlements; 3. Small settlements.

Administrative hierarchy No evidence for administrative hierarchy; may have had completely different political organisation than what is seen in other ancient urban societies, ie a heterarchical organisation.

Institutions

Legal code No data

Bureaucracy No data

Religious validation of rule No clear evidence for rulers

Property rights No data

Price controls No data

Banking regulations No data

Economy

Taxation Probably absent. No evidence for state organisation.

Coinage Absent

Credit No data

Agricultural practices

Main crop Rice

Irrigation Probably absent

Fertilising Probably absent

Cropping system Two-field rotation

Metallurgy

Base metal Iron

Military equipment

Handheld weapons Clubs and spears existed, but it is unclear whether they were used in warfare.

Armour No evidence for armour

Projectiles Bows and spears existed, but it is unclear whether they
    were used in warfare.

Incendiaries No evidence

Long walls No evidence

Well-being

Life expectancy No data

Average adult stature No data

Irrigation & drinking water Unclear. Rice cultivated, but irrigation
    probably unnecessary due to natural flooding of the Niger Inland
    Delta; however, irrigation technology known in sub-Saharan
    Africa by this time; drinking water probably taken from rivers.

Health care No data. No evidence for this, but apparent absence of
    a centralised state does not preclude existence of welfare
    services.

Alimentary support No data. No evidence for this, but apparent
    absence of a centralised state does not preclude existence of
    welfare services.

Famine relief No data. No evidence for this, but apparent absence of
    a centralised state does not preclude existence of welfare
    services.

(In)equalities

Social mobility Probably present. Evidence of poor labourers gaining
    wealth and prominence, sometimes through marriage.

Occupational mobility Probably absent

Gender equality No data

Slavery Unclear. Evidence for bonded labour, probably not chattel
    slavery.

Human sacrifice Probably absent

Religion

Majority religious practice Jenné-jenno religion. Clay figurines depicting animals and humans in various poses offer a tantalising glimpse into an obscure belief system.

Iran: Parthian Empire

Founded by the Parnis, a nomadic eastern-Iranian people who revolted against Seleucid rule, the Parthian Empire covered much of Southwest Asia, including Babylonia, which the Parni conquered around 141 BCE. The empire was large and diverse, encompassing practitioners of Zoroastrianism, Greco-Macedonian and Egyptian polytheism, South Asian Brahminic and Buddhist thought, and West Asian Judaism, all coexisting relatively peacefully. Over time, rivalry with Rome (and perhaps the empire's sheer size) led to it fracturing. In 226 CE it fell to the Sassanids, a dynasty from the mountainous regions of southwestern Iran.

General
Duration 247 BCE–244 CE
Languages Pahlavi (Indo-European); Greek (Indo-European)
Preceded by Seleucid kingdom
Succeeded by Sassanid Empire

Territory
Total area (km²) 280,000 in 200 BCE; 2m in 100 BCE; 3m in 1 CE; 1.9m in 100 CE; 1.8m in 200 CE.

People
Population 5.45m in 100 BCE; 7.5–15m in 1 CE; 4.75m in 100 CE; 5m in 200 CE. (Estimates, due to lack of empire-wide census.)
Largest city 600,000 (Seleucia-Ctesiphon)
Standing army 300,000

Social scale

Settlement hierarchy 1. Multiple capitals; 2. Major regional centres; 3. Towns; 4. Villages; 5. Hamlets.

Administrative hierarchy 1. King; 2. First minister; 3. Department heads (*dibirs*); 4. Regional governors (*satraps*); 5. Minor administrative officials and scribes.

Institutions

Legal code Mixed. Empire divided into self-governing regions with their own legal codes; unclear whether a law code existed in the Parthian heartland.

Bureaucracy Based on Achaemenid system; government offices (*divans*) kept records and dealt with state financial matters.

Religious validation of rule King seen as representative of the gods on earth.

Property rights There was a class of land-owning farmers.

Price controls Mixed. May well have been enforced by self-governing regional authorities; no evidence for centralised price control.

Banking regulations Already present in much of the empire's territory before the Parthian conquest.

Economy

Taxation Land and head taxes in the cities; taxes on trade; special religious collections; could be paid in kind.

Coinage Gold and silver drachm

Credit Private banks offering range of services existed from 600 BCE.

Agricultural practices

Main crops Wheat and barley

Irrigation Present

Fertilising Manuring

Cropping system Fallowing, two-field rotation and nitrogen-fixing crops.

Metallurgy

Base metals Bronze, iron and steel

Military equipment

Handheld weapons Cataphracts (heavy cavalry) used 12-foot *kontos*
(lance); swords, axes, maces and daggers known as secondary
weapons.

Armour Helmets, breastplates, limb and neck protectors, lamellar,
scale, plate and chain-mail armour; horses also wore felt or
leather protection.

Projectiles Composite bows

Incendiaries Naphtha bombs

Long walls No evidence

Well-being

Life expectancy No data

Average adult stature No data

Irrigation & drinking water Mixed. Irrigation system present long
before Parthian conquest; *qanat* system brought drinking water
in many areas.

Health care Evidence for underground sewerage in certain buildings.
Long-standing tradition of professional medicine throughout
area, pre-dating Parthian conquest.

Alimentary support Mixed. May have existed for self-governing
regions; no evidence for a centralised system.

Famine relief Mixed. May have existed for self-governing regions;
there were royal storehouses but no evidence for a centralised
famine relief system.

(In)equalities

Social mobility Limited. Administrative roles open to non-Parthians;
over time, positions of greatest power became hereditary;
distinction developed between landowners and landless.

Occupational mobility Tax-paying labourers allowed to change occupation; at the elite level, certain positions were monopolised by powerful families.

Gender equality Ideology fostered gender inequality throughout the empire, but women could divorce (with husband's consent) and remarry.

Slavery War captives made to work on large construction projects.

Human sacrifice Absent. Forbidden by Zoroastrianism.

Religion

Majority religious practices Zoroastrianism. Christianity, Judaism and Mithraism also practised.

Mongolia: Xiongnu confederacy

The Xiongnu confederacy comprised several nomadic peoples from the Mongolian steppe. By the 4th century BCE, the Xiongnu began raiding northern China. Their mounted archery overwhelmed the heavily armed but relatively immobile Chinese infantry and triggered early attempts at building a "Great Wall" in northern China. The nomads were held at bay by a combination of tribute in the form of metals, finished products and agricultural products, and China's superiority in numbers. Several Chinese victories against the Xiongnu in the 1st century CE and factional conflict within the confederacy led to the confederacy's break-up, and a new group of semi-nomadic peoples from the northeast, the Xianbei, took control of the region.

General
Duration 209 BCE–100 CE
Language Xiongnu (probably Turkic)
Preceded by Early Xiongnu peoples
Succeeded by Xianbei confederacy

Territory
Total area (km²) 4m

People
Population 1.5m
Largest city Ivolga had c. 3,000 inhabitants but it was probably not the largest settlement; capital remains unidentified.
Standing army 300,000

Social scale

Settlement hierarchy 1. Permanent settlements; 2. Seasonal settlements; 3. Campsites.

Administrative hierarchy 1. Supreme leader (Chanyu); 2. Lesser rulers; 3. Tribal Xiongnu chiefs; 4. Non-Xiongnu chiefs.

Institutions

Legal code Unclear. Chinese chronicles recognised a simple and strict system of law but it was not written down.

Bureaucracy Absent

Religious validation of rule Chanyu was believed to be supported by the supreme god, Tengri.

Property rights No data

Price controls Absent

Banking regulations Absent

Economy

Taxation Chanyu expected tribute from lesser rulers and coerced his subjects into forced labour.

Coinage Absent

Credit Absent

Agricultural practices

Main crop None; grain was obtained by trading or raiding.

Irrigation Absent

Fertilising Absent

Cropping system Animal husbandry, seasonal harvesting

Metallurgy

Base metals Bronze, iron and steel

Military equipment
Handheld weapons War clubs, battle axes, swords, daggers and
    spears.
Armour Wooden shields and leather helmets; metal armour
    (including chain mail, scale and plate armour) may have spread
    from Western steppes.
Projectiles Composite bows
Incendiaries No evidence
Long walls Absent

Well-being
Life expectancy No data
Average adult stature No data
Irrigation & drinking water Absent
Health care Absent. Medical services provided by shamans.
Alimentary support Absent
Famine relief Indications of support given to fellow tribesmen

(In)equalities
Social mobility Hereditary elite
Occupational mobility Absent. Men were often full-time warriors.
Gender equality One contemporary Chinese writer said the Xiongnu
    "make no distinction between men and women".
Slavery Present
Human sacrifice Enslaved people, concubines and war captives killed
    as part of elite men's funerals.

Religion
Majority religious practices Xiongnu religion; early Tengrism.
    Animist belief in spirits; shamans practised sorcery and
    divination.

China: Western Han Empire

The Western Han Empire was founded in 202 BCE when Liu Bang, a charismatic commoner from the former state of Han, led a rebellion against the short-lived Qin dynasty, which ruled much of northern and central China. The Han expanded Chinese control north into Central Asia, east to Manchuria and northern Korea, and south to northern Vietnam. The empire is known for its economic, technological and artistic achievements, strong state control and promulgation of Confucian thought – centuries old by this period – as state-sponsored ideology, at times using exams based on Confucian principles to recruit civil servants. Former military general and regent Wang Mang ended the dynasty in 9 CE, claiming the throne for himself.

General
Duration 202 BCE–9 CE
Language Chinese (Sino-Tibetan)
Preceded by Imperial Qin
Succeeded by Eastern Han

Territory
Total area (km²) 2.4m in 200 BCE; 4.5m in 100 BCE; 4.9m in 1 CE

People
Population 45m–60m in 200 BCE; 57.6m in 1 CE
Largest city 250,000–300,000 (Chang'an)
Standing army 100,000–200,000

Social scale

Settlement hierarchy 1. Capital (Chang'an); 2. Commandery capital;
3. District capital; 4. Foreign vassal city; 5. Medium-sized
settlement; 6. Small settlement.

Administrative hierarchy 1. Emperor; 2. Top administrators; 3. Bureau
heads; 4. Division heads; 5. Sub-heads; 6. Lower-level officials;
7. On-site supervisors.

Institutions

Legal code Same code as Imperial Qin, minus some of the more
severe measures.

Bureaucracy At the turn of the millennium the Chinese bureaucracy
was highly departmentalised and employed over 100,000
officials throughout China.

Religious validation of rule Mandate of Heaven: Emperor's role was to
ensure appeasement or favour of the Supreme Power (*Di*).

Property rights Limited. In principle, all land was owned by
Emperor; in practice, private-type rights were exercised over
land. Many nobles held fief-like authority over territory and
communities of labourers.

Price controls Commodity price equalisation was often attempted;
price inflation was suppressed by release of stored surplus and
increased through purchase and additional storage.

Banking regulations Probably present

Economy

Taxation Taxes on agricultural production and the sale of goods; poll
tax; tribute from nobles and dependent kings.

Coinage Billions of coins, called *wu zhu*, were minted during the
Western Han dynasty and stayed in circulation for nearly a
millennium.

/kingdoms; 4. Cities; 5. Tributary communities; 6. Villages
; 7. Rural settlements (*pagi*).

strative hierarchy 1. Emperor; 2. Imperial officials (eg
aestores); 3. Provincial governors (*proconsules*); 4. Senior
rovincial officials (eg *praetores*); 5. Provincial staff (*lictores*);
. Municipal magistrates (eg *duoviri*); 7. Public slaves and
servants.

stitutions

Legal code Formal legal code first founded in the Twelve Tables of
450–449 BCE. Law thereafter was based on precedent.

Bureaucracy Professional/volunteer. Most administrative duties
filled by citizen volunteers or compulsory service. Some full-
time salaried officials.

Religious validation of rule Emperors legitimated directly by religious
activity or considered ordained to rule by gods. Emperors
performed many ritual activities and often served as high priest.
Emperors in Eastern Mediterranean worshipped as gods.

Property rights Full rights to private property ownership: usufruct,
exclusivity, partibility, right to lease and right to sell. No
prescribed use of property by state.

Price controls Largely absent. No regular limits to market prices. At
extraordinary times price limits were set (eg 19 CE ceiling to
price of grain in Rome imposed by Emperor Tiberius).

Banking regulations Absent. No formal control or limitations to
banking practice.

Economy

Taxation Coin and in-kind taxes; collected on land, people,
commerce and movement.

Coinage 1 gold (*aureus*) = 4 silver (*denarii*) = 100 bronze (*sestertii*).

Credit Loans mainly from wealthy individuals to other members of
their class.

Agricultural practices

Main crops Millet. Wheat also cultivated; rice cultivated in south.

Irrigation Present

Fertilising Present

Cropping system Crop rotation

Metallurgy

Base metals Bronze, iron and steel

Military equipment

Handheld weapons Spears, halberds, dagger-axes, war clubs, daggers
and swords.

Armour Breastplates, cuirasses, helmets and limb protection; leather
and iron lamellar armour used by infantry; shields used by
cavalry but uncommon.

Projectiles Bows and crossbows

Incendiaries Petroleum-based incendiary bombs

Long walls Expansion of long walls in north; beginnings of Great
Wall.

Well-being

Life expectancy 20 years from birth

Average adult stature 166 cm (male); 157 cm (female)

Irrigation & drinking water Irrigation encouraged by the Han to
increase crop yields; wells, reservoirs, canals and aqueducts
present; however, no large-scale pipe networks.

Health care No data

Alimentary support Western Han gave landless peasants royal land
grants and encouraged aristocracy to do the same.

Famine relief Commandery-level authorities provided food; imperial administrators provided tax relief and gifts.

(In)equalities

Social mobility Examination system enabled male commoners to attain administrative roles.

Occupational mobility Present

Gender equality Administrative roles closed to women, but a will dating to 5 CE suggests that a widow could own land.

Slavery War captives enslaved; common also to enslave debtors and relatives of criminals.

Human sacrifice War captives often sacrificed, despite Confucian scholars' disapproval.

Religion

Majority religious practices Chinese folk religion; Confucianism; Daoism.

Italy: Roman Principate

The Roman Principate refers to the first ⸢ Empire, when the Emperor was termed *princeps,* Beginning with the victory of the first empero⸢ Octavian), over Mark Antony and the Egyptian que⸢ 31 BCE, the Principate became one of the largest, m⸢ and most prosperous imperial states ever known. It ⸢ this period that Rome built the Pantheon, the Colosseum, ⸢ temples and public markets in the heart of Rome, and man⸢ important buildings. Rome underwent crisis along with adm⸢ trative and economic reforms in the mid-3rd century (235–84 ⸢ inaugurating a second phase of the empire, the Dominate.

General

Duration 31 BCE–284 CE

Languages Latin (Indo-European); Ancient Greek (Indo-European)

Preceded by Roman Republic

Succeeded by Roman Dominate

Territory

Total area (km²) 4.5m in 1 CE; 5.8m in 100 CE; 4.75m in 275 CE

People

Population 50m in 1 CE; 50–60m in 100 CE

Largest city 1m (Rome: 1st–3rd century CE)

Standing army 250,000–400,000

Social scale

Settlement hierarchy 1. Capital (Rome); 2. Provincial centres; 3. Client

Numerous lower bronze denominations; 8.4 lb wheat cost roughly 4–6 *sestertii*.

Credit Banking, notional credit and deposit accounts known. Wages: 900 *sestertii* (soldier, 1st century CE); 1,200 *sestertii* (soldier, 2nd century CE).

Agricultural practices

Main crops Wheat, olives and grapes

Irrigation Present

Fertilising Present

Cropping system Crop rotation, nitrogen-fixing crops and short-fallowing.

Metallurgy

Base metals Copper, bronze and iron

Military equipment

Handheld weapons Daggers, swords and spears

Armour Breastplates, shields, helmets, limb coverings, scaled armour and plate armour.

Projectiles Javelins, slings, self-bows, composite bows and crossbows.

Incendiaries Pitch on siege engines

Long walls 119 km (Hadrian's Wall, Britain in 123 CE)

Well-being

Life expectancy 25.3 years from birth

Average adult stature 164 cm (male); 155 cm (female)

Irrigation & drinking water Aqueducts were common throughout the empire, built and maintained by public means (both state and local level) and often by private citizens.

Health care Designated areas for healing existed, especially spa-like

treatment areas (eg Aesclepeion on Tiber Island in Rome), but
were not common or systematically maintained.

Alimentary support Free distribution of grain in the city of Rome to
poor citizens (the *annona*), from 58 BCE to the end of the 4th
century CE. In the early 3rd century CE olive oil was added to the
distribution.

Famine relief Mixed. No public funds earmarked for relief. Emperor
and wealthy elite individuals provided free or subsidised food to
needy citizens in times of famine on an ad hoc basis.

(In)equalities

Social mobility Hereditary elite status, with mobility especially
among wealthy provincial citizens and military officers.

Occupational mobility Present. Hereditary adoption of certain crafts
(textiles, ceramics) but no strict legal or cultural restrictions.

Gender equality Legal distinction between men and women. Women
could be priests and own property but not hold military or
political office.

Slavery Chattel slavery prevalent. Enslaved people were mostly war
captives, children born to enslaved parents, and people sold into
slavery (to pay off debts, for example); 7–15% of the population
was enslaved.

Human sacrifice Absent

Religion

Majority religious practices Ancient Roman paganism. Worship of a
pantheon of deities, as was common to Mediterranean peoples
in general; Judaism (practised by a minority); Christianity
(emerged in early 1st century CE, spread throughout Principate
thereafter).

Afghanistan: Kushan Empire

The Kushan Empire rose from a Parthian vassal kingdom in Bactria to become a powerful imperial confederation uniting groups from Uzbekistan, Afghanistan, Pakistan and northern India. An absolute monarchy with strong centralised ideological and military control, it maintained an uneasy but stable co-existence with the Parthians to the west. Kushan coins appear throughout the region, revealing strong trade links. These extended to the cultural sphere as well: the Kushans adapted Zoroastrianism along with aspects of Greek polytheism as well as Shaivism, Jainism, Vaishnavism and Buddhism as they extended their control and contact with the subcontinent. In the mid-3rd century CE, the Sassanids overran both the Kushans and the Parthian Empire.

General
Duration 35–370 CE
Languages Bactrian (Indo-European); Gandhari (Indo-European)
Preceded by Tocharians; Greco-Bactrian kingdom
Succeeded by Sassanid Empire

Territory
Total area (km²) 2m–2.5m

People
Population 12.5m–13.5m in 100 CE; 14m–15m in 200 CE
Largest city 150,000 in 100 CE (Taxila); 100,000 in 200 CE (Merv)
Standing army Less than 100,000 according to Chinese texts, though this might refer only to infantry.

Social scale

Settlement hierarchy 1. Capital (Purashapura); 2. Regional capitals
(Taxila, Begram, Mathura); 3. Towns; 4. Rural settlements;
5. Nomadic camps.

Administrative hierarchy 1. King; 2. Regional governors (*satraps*);
3. Regional officials (*dandanayakas*); 4. Village chiefs (*gramas* or
pradapalas).

Institutions

Legal code Probably present. Legal documents have been recovered.

Bureaucracy Professional. Salaried officials mostly known to operate
at lower levels.

Religious validation of rule According to official ideology, the king
was a god who drew his power from other gods.

Property rights No data

Price controls Absent

Banking regulations Absent

Economy

Taxation No data

Coinage Kushan bronze and gold coins; Roman coins also used.

Credit The Kushans introduced a long-lasting banking system in
northern India.

Agricultural practices

Main crops Wheat and barley; rice in some areas

Irrigation Present

Fertilising Present

Cropping system Mixed. Fallowing, crop rotation known in some
regions.

Metallurgy

Base metals Bronze, iron and steel

Military equipment

Handheld weapons War clubs, maces, battle axes, daggers, long and short swords, cataphract lances, infantry spears, tridents and halberds.

Armour Shields, helmets, iron breastplates, leg and arm protectors, chain mail, scaled and plate armour (including muscle cuirass).

Projectiles Slings, simple bows, composite bows and crossbows

Incendiaries No evidence

Long walls Northern border ran along pre-existing wall built to divide Bactria region from Sogdia.

Well-being

Life expectancy No data

Average adult stature No data

Irrigation & drinking water Extensive irrigation system in crop-growing areas of Central Asia; city-dwellers drew water from wells.

Health care No centralised medical system; health-care services probably provided by Buddhist institutions.

Alimentary support Absent. Probably provided by Buddhist institutions; possibly also by regional or city authorities.

Famine relief Absent. Probably provided by Buddhist institutions; possibly also by regional or city authorities.

(In)equalities

Social mobility Mixed. Social mobility probably highest in prosperous trade hubs in Gandhara, lowest in Indian territories due to caste system.

Occupational mobility Mixed. Flourishing trade created new jobs for merchants, priests in temples and craft professionals; Central Asian peasants not bound to land; in Indian territories, caste system.

Gender equality Elite women could attain positions of power and
influence; records show they could be educated, and wealthy
enough to donate to religious institutions.

Slavery Widespread; traded with Rome.

Human sacrifice Probably present. Not common practice in any
major religion present in the Kushan Empire.

Religion

Majority religious practices Mahayana Buddhism; Saivite Hinduism;
Ancient Greek religion; Zoroastrianism.

Cambodia: Funan kingdom

"Funan" is a name given by contemporary Chinese sources to what they perceived as an extensive centralised kingdom, but which modern historians believe was a collection of several small kingdoms in the monsoon area of Southeast Asia, covering parts of what is today Vietnam, Thailand and Cambodia. Funan prospered in its privileged position at the crossroads of important trade routes around the South China Sea: in effect, a maritime Silk Road. The wealth of Funan was exhibited in, and supported by, large-scale public works and infrastructure projects, including an extensive series of canals, drainage works, roads and markets. The Funanese disintegrated in the early 7th century. The kingdom known by Chinese sources as Zhenla originating further up the Mekong river rose in its stead.

General
Duration 225–639 CE
Languages Unclear (Austroasiatic); probably related to Mon and/or Khmer.
Preceded by Early Mekong Delta peoples
Succeeded by Zhenla kingdom

Territory
Total area (km²) 250,000–300,000

People
Population 100,000–200,000
Largest city 2,000 (Angkor Borei)

Standing army No data. Chinese records suggest that the temple on
Ling-kia-po-pho mountain was permanently guarded by a
thousand soldiers, but this may well have been only a fraction of
the total army, and the records' reliability is unclear.

Social scale

Settlement hierarchy 1. Large ceremonial centre (Angkor Borei);
2. Medium-sized village; 3. Small village.

Administrative hierarchy 1. *Pon* (head) of large village; 2. *Pon* of
medium-sized village; 3. *Pon* of small village.

Institutions

Legal code Imported from India.

Bureaucracy Unclear. Inscriptions from the 7th century onwards
include references to figures such as an "inspector of royal
property".

Religious validation of rule *Pons* inherited their right to rule through
their mother's line.

Property rights *Pons* owned land, but so did commoner men and
women; some land had multiple owners.

Price controls Absent

Banking regulations No data

Economy

Taxation Taxes were imposed on valuable commodities such as gold,
silver, perfumes, semi-precious stones and pearls.

Coinage Probably absent. Experts disagree, but it is worth noting
that archaeological excavations have retrieved only two coins,
one of them Roman.

Credit Unclear

Agricultural practices

Main crop Rice

Irrigation Present
Fertilising Absent
Cropping system Swidden farming and short-fallowing, with
intensive wet-rice farming.

Metallurgy
Base metals Bronze and iron

Military equipment
Handheld weapons Knives, spears and swords; probably iron battle
axes later known as *phka'k*.
Armour Possible bronze helmets found; probably some armour
made of perishable material.
Projectiles Javelins and bows
Incendiaries No evidence
Long walls No evidence

Well-being
Life expectancy No data
Average adult stature Unclear. At the site of Phum Snay, men had an
average height of 166.5 cm and women 155 cm; however, this site
was not part of Funan.
Irrigation & drinking water LiDAR scans show major irrigation
networks, including many large canals, dating from the 5th
century CE. Reservoirs known as *barays* were also constructed.
Health care Unclear. Temples may have provided a simple health-
care service.
Alimentary support Unclear. Temples may have provided alimentary
support to the poor.
Famine relief Provided by temples.

(In)equalities
Social mobility Hereditary elite status

Occupational mobility Absent

Gender equality At least some women enjoyed high status and a role in public life, but only men could become *pons*.

Slavery Enslaved people were primarily war captives.

Human sacrifice Chinese records say that the *pon* himself performed human sacrifice at Ling-kia-po-pho temple.

Religion

Majority religious practices Saivite Hinduism; Mahayana Buddhism

Japan: Kofun

Centred in the Kansai region around the Nara basin and Osaka plain in present-day Japan, the Kofun culture was not a unitary, centralised state but a shared cultural sphere linking several independent regional groups. The Kofun period is notable for the widespread use of keyhole-shaped burial mounds known as *kofun*, and temples and artefacts relating to a shamanistic and animistic religion, practices that eventually morphed into what we know as Japanese Shinto. By the mid-6th century CE, the influence of Buddhist thought from China and Chinese-style legal and administrative forms changed the prevailing culture enough that modern scholars designate this new phase the Asuka period.

General
Duration 250–538 CE
Language Old Japanese (Japonic)
Preceded by Yayoi period
Succeeded by Asuka period

Territory
Total area (km²) 10,000–15,000. (Estimate, based on extent of material culture finds.)

People
Population 150,000–300,000
Largest city Unclear
Standing army No data

Social scale
Settlement hierarchy 1. Large settlements; 2. Medium-sized settlements; 3. Small settlements.
Administrative hierarchy 1. Ruler; 2. Top officials; 3. Incipient administration.

Institutions
Legal code Probably absent
Bureaucracy Unclear. First emergence of an administrative system, but very poorly understood.
Religious validation of rule Beginning in the 4th century CE, rulers were believed to be gods.
Property rights Reallocation of rice paddies to government in 645 CE suggests that previously they may have been privately held.
Price controls No data
Banking regulations No data

Economy
Taxation No data
Coinage Coins found in archaeological excavations, but their use remains unclear.
Credit Probably absent

Agricultural practices
Main crops Rice; barley also cultivated.
Irrigation Present
Fertilising Probably absent
Cropping system Uncertain. May have used two-field rotation.

Metallurgy
Base metals Bronze and iron

Military equipment
Handheld weapons Battle axes, daggers, swords, spears and polearms
Armour Padded armour made of cloth, shields and breastplates; laminar armour from the 4th century; helmets from the 5th century.
Projectiles Javelins, sling shots and simple bows
Incendiaries No evidence
Long walls No evidence

Well-being
Life expectancy No data
Average adult stature 161.5 cm (male); 150 cm (female)
Irrigation & drinking water Present
Health care No data
Alimentary support Village-owned storehouses
Famine relief Village-owned storehouses

(In)equalities
Social mobility Hereditary elite
Occupational mobility Absent. Occupational choice limited to location and birth.
Gender equality Some Kofun-era chieftains were women.
Slavery Not widespread; enslaved population made up of prisoners of war and their descendants, criminals, debtors, and children sold by their parents.
Human sacrifice Probably absent. Most experts do not believe human sacrifice was performed at this time.

Religion
Majority religious practice Early Shinto

Medieval: 500 to 1500 CE

France: Merovingian kingdom

When the Western Roman Empire fell and her political authority
vanished, many former provinces re-formed into medium-sized
kingdoms maintaining Roman forms of governance; the Merovingian
kingdom was one such. The Merovingians were in many ways a
typical medieval European "feudal" society, with the king ruling
over a loose hierarchy of semi-autonomous nobles. The capital
was at Paris, where the population may have reached 30,000 by the
8th century CE. In other respects, the Merovingians maintained
continuity with their Roman predecessors, such as with their hybrid
legal system based on Roman precedent, with statutes and rescripts
written in Latin, though they increasingly incorporated elements of
Germanic culture and language. In 752 CE, the Carolingians deposed
the Merovingian's Frankish ruling dynasty, establishing the Carolingian kingdom.

General
Duration 481–751 CE
Languages Romance Latin (Indo-European); Frankish (Indo-
    European).
Preceded by Roman Dominate
Succeeded by Carolingian kingdom

Territory
Total area (km²) 600,000 in 500 CE; 1.5m in 650 CE

People
Population 7m

Largest city 20,000–30,000 (Paris)

Standing army Unknown. 5,000–6,000 soldiers generally fielded in military engagements.

Social scale
Settlement hierarchy 1. Capital (Paris); 2. Cities; 3. Towns; 4. Farmsteads.

Administrative hierarchy 1. King; 2. Court officials (eg Mayor of the Palace); 3. Court administrators; 4. Regional officials (dukes and bishops); 5. City-district officials (counts); 6. Minor city officials (eg *rachinburgi*, in charge of law).

Institutions
Legal code The earliest surviving Frankish law code is the *Pactus legis Salicae* or Salic law, which was compiled around 500 CE by King Clovis.

Bureaucracy Absent

Religious validation of rule King appointed by pope, though based on lineage descent. Rulers seen as representatives of God on earth.

Property rights No data

Price controls Absent

Banking regulations Absent

Economy
Taxation Taxes on property (including wheeled vehicles), tolls (eg bridge dues) and land.

Coinage From 550s CE onwards, gold Merovingian coins were used, modelled on the Roman *solidus*; the coin was progressively debased with silver until replaced with the silver *denarius* in the 660s CE.

Credit Gallo-Roman historian Gregory of Tours wrote that Jewish merchants provided loans to the Merovingian kings in the form of bonds secured on public taxation.

Agricultural practices
Main crop Wheat
Irrigation Present
Fertilising Absent
Cropping system Two-field rotation

Metallurgy
Base metals Bronze, iron and steel

Military equipment
Handheld weapons Spears, one-handed battle axes, scramasaxes (a type of dagger), double-edged long swords, lances and short swords.

Armour Shields, helmets, limb protection, chain mail, laminar armour and padding; materials included wood, cloth, leather and iron.

Projectiles Javelins, *angos* (iron throwing-spears), *franciscas* (heavy throwing-axe), slings and simple short bows.

Incendiaries No evidence
Long walls No evidence

Well-being
Life expectancy 30 years from birth
Average adult stature 167.6 cm (male); 154 cm (female)
Irrigation & drinking water At the local level, churches maintained Roman aqueducts, water-supply systems and irrigation canals.

Health care Mixed. Not at state level, but some basic health care provided by monasteries.

Alimentary support Provided by the church; king also expected to demonstrate largesse in lean times.

Famine relief Provided by the church.

(In)equalities

Social mobility Hereditary elite

Occupational mobility Absent. Largely restricted to the elite.

Gender equality Male-dominated society; aristocratic women could gain some form of power and autonomy by climbing the church hierarchy.

Slavery Not widespread but mentioned in records, including Salic law and records of church land.

Human sacrifice Absent. Certain pre-Christian rituals involving human sacrifice may have survived, but the act was forbidden by the church.

Religion

Majority religious practice Roman Catholicism. This became the state religion after King Clovis's baptism in 508 CE.

Turkey: Byzantine Empire

The Byzantine Empire remains one of history's longest-lasting states. Emerging as an eastern reorientation of the Roman Empire, the so-called Byzantines saw themselves as ruling over an unbroken Roman Empire, rather than something new. The early period is often termed Eastern Roman Empire, while the name for the latter period was given by modern historians after the Greek city of Byzantium – refounded in the 4th century as the new capital city of Constantinople, today Istanbul – which sat in an advantageous position at the junction of sea and land routes. The Christian "Byzantine" emperor (self-described as a Roman) was its chief lawmaker and military commander as well as the church's leading patron, though religious matters were often contested. The Bishop of Rome (later known as the pope) and other powerful bishops competed with the emperor for ideological and political supremacy; indeed, the stated aim of several of Western Christendom's Crusades was to compel the Byzantines to submit to papal authority. Some date the beginning of the Byzantine Empire to 395 CE, when the Roman Empire was officially partitioned into Western and Eastern halves, though we focus here on the period beginning in the mid-7th century, after the fall of the Western Roman Empire and the rise of the early Islamic caliphates saw a more distinctly "Byzantine" society develop. Constantinople's walls were finally breached in 1453 CE by Ottoman Sultan Mehmed II.

General
Duration 632–1453 CE
Languages Greek (Indo-European); Latin (Indo-European)

Preceded by Eastern Roman Empire

Succeeded by Ottoman Empire

Territory

Total area (km²) 1.3m–2m in 600 CE; 470,000–700,000 in 700;
520,000–650,000 in 800; 610,000 in 900; 810,000 in 1000;
750,000 in 1100; 480,000–600,000 in 1200; 200,000 in 1300;
30,000 in 1400.

People

Population 15–17m in 600 CE; 4.5–7m in 700; 5–8m in 800; 8m in
900; 12m in 1000; 5–10m in 1100; 7–9m in 1200; 2m in 1300.

Largest city 150,000 in 600 CE; 80,000–125,000 in 700; 100,000–
350,000 in 800; 100,000–300,000 in 900; 200,000–300,000 in
1000; 250,000 in 1100; 150,000–300,000 in 1200; 100,000–
250,000 in 1300 (Constantinople).

Standing army 80,000–120,000 in 632–866 CE; 150,000 in 900;
250,000–325,000 in 1000; 100,000–150,000 in 1100; 100,000–
150,000 in 1200.

Social scale

Settlement hierarchy 1. Capital (Constantinople); 2. Provincial
capitals; 3. Provincial cities; 4. Provincial towns; 5. Villages
(*chorion*); 6. Hamlets (*agridia*).

Administrative hierarchy 1. Emperor (*Basileus*); 2. First minister
(*logothete* of the *dromos*); 3. General fiscal supervisor (*sakellarios*);
4. Military finance and general treasury officials; 5. Provincial
military administrators; 6. Provincial financial administrators;
7. Lesser provincial officials; 8. Staff in public offices.

Institutions

Legal code *Codex Justinianus*. Compiled in Latin, later translated into
Ancient Greek.

Bureaucracy Professional

Religious validation of rule The *Basileus* was God's elect on earth, though depended on acceptance of army officials, senators and people in the capital; cult of the emperor was in evidence.

Property rights The *Codex Justinianus* as a sum of Roman legal precedent included a number of provisions regarding private property rights.

Price controls Present

Banking regulations The state regulated interest rates, banned money-lending and money-changing.

Economy

Taxation Taxes on land, property, trade and agricultural production.

Coinage The average monthly wage of an unskilled labourer was 1 *nomisma* (a gold coin weighing 4.55 g), which was enough to feed and clothe a family, as well as pay rent on a small house. In the period under consideration, a *modios thalassios* of wheat (12.8 kg) oscillated considerably, reaching 1/60 of a *nomisma* at its very lowest and 1 *nomisma* at its highest.

Credit Highly regulated by the state.

Agricultural practices

Main crops Wheat, olives and grapes

Irrigation Present

Fertilising Present

Cropping system Nitrogen-fixing crops

Metallurgy

Base metals Bronze, iron and steel

Military equipment

Handheld weapons Iron maces, swords (*spathion*), daggers, spears and polearms; elite Rus' and Nordic Varangian guard mercenaries wielded axes.

Armour Body and limb protection made of silk, cotton, felt and metal (eg iron helmets and bronze leg greaves); chain mail over fabric protection; shields.

Projectiles Javelins, sling shots and composite bows; mounted crossbows were used on the battlefield and in siege situations.

Incendiaries Greek fire projectors, mounted and hand-held.

Long walls 60-km-long walls built to the west of Constantinople

Well-being

Life expectancy 30–45 years from birth (male); 25–35 years (female)

Average adult stature 161–178 cm (male); 146–162 cm (female)

Irrigation & drinking water Irrigation mostly used for cash crops in Greece and Turkey; 70 underground and open-air cisterns and a 500-km-long network of aqueducts provided 1 million m³ of drinking water to Constantinople.

Health care State-funded and privately funded homes for the elderly poor, orphanages, infirmaries and hospitals.

Alimentary support State-funded almshouses (*xenodocheia*).

Famine relief Relatively extensive welfare services, though these were expanded or curtailed under different emperors.

(In)equalities

Social mobility Bureaucracy and court milieu relatively open to "outsiders", regardless of class or ethnicity.

Occupational mobility Limited, especially within church administration.

Gender equality Married women maintained power of disposal over dowries, especially in cases of divorce. Widows were able to escape some constraints and some elite women wielded

significant political influence. In other respects, women were
under the legal authority of husbands or fathers.

Slavery Chattel slavery; most enslaved people were either war
captives, people who entered the empire enslaved, or the
descendants of enslaved people; worth noting that enslaved
people had relatively extensive rights, including ones of property
and inheritance.

Human sacrifice Absent. Forbidden by Christianity.

Religion

Majority religious practice Eastern Catholicism; Eastern Orthodox
Christianity starting in 1054 CE, after the estrangement and Great
Schism between church leaders in Rome and Constantinople due
to controversies over jurisdictional authority and matters of
orthodoxy.

Uzbekistan: Sogdian city-states

Sometimes referred to by the names of their principal cities, Bukhara and Samarkand, the Sogdian city-states occupied a region now split between Afghanistan, Uzbekistan, Turkmenistan and Tajikistan. Cities in Zarafshan and surrounding valleys carved independent zones out of Sassanid territory and competed to control trade. The mid-7th century CE, when Samarkand was at its peak, saw the appearance of large walled palaces and richly decorated necropolises. Perhaps due to its strategic spot along the Silk Road, the region was home to many cultures, including Zoroastrianism, Nestorian Christianity, Buddhism and Judaism. The period ended in the early 8th century when the Umayyad caliphate conquered the region.

General
Duration 604–711 CE
Language Sogdian (Indo-European)
Preceded by Western Turk khaganate
Succeeded by Umayyad caliphate; Tang dynasty

Territory
Total area (km²) 10,000–20,000. This is roughly the size of the region incorporating the various city-states.

People
Population Unknown
Largest city The population of Samarkand is not known, but an estimate of 40,000 is not unreasonable.

Standing army No data

Social scale
Settlement hierarchy 1. City-state; 2. Satellite towns; 3. Villages.
Administrative hierarchy 1. King and/or merchant council; 2. Central administration; 3. Lesser officials; 4. Local authorities.

Institutions
Legal code Sogdian legal texts have not survived but are known to have existed from an inscription; likely to have been largely concerned with trade regulations.
Bureaucracy Professional
Religious validation of rule Likely to have been through ritual and religion.
Property rights No data
Price controls No data
Banking regulations No data

Economy
Taxation Probably present
Coinage Barter prevalent, but Samarkand minted cast bronze coins with a square hole in the middle to function as a unit of account; Sassanid silver coins also in use.
Credit Based on the importance of trade and merchants.

Agricultural practices
Main crops Wheat and barley
Irrigation Present
Fertilising Probably absent
Cropping system Unclear

Metallurgy
Base metals Bronze and iron

Military equipment

Handheld weapons War clubs, battle axes, daggers, swords and lances.

Armour Leather-covered wooden shields, helmets, breastplates, limb protection, chain mail, scaled and laminar armour.

Projectiles Javelins, composite bows, Persian nawaks or tubebows

Incendiaries Grenades with sulphur, asphalt and naphtha, particularly in sieges.

Long walls Not known to have been built.

Well-being

Life expectancy No data

Average adult stature No data

Irrigation & drinking water Samarkand's water supply came from reservoirs delivered into the city by canals and to individual properties through clay pipes.

Health care Unclear. Possibly provided by Zoroastrian temples.

Alimentary support Unclear. Possibly provided by Zoroastrian temples.

Famine relief Unclear. Possibly provided by Zoroastrian temples.

(In)equalities

Social mobility No data

Occupational mobility No data

Gender equality No data

Slavery Chattel slavery; merchants and aristocrats owned enslaved people responsible for the security and administration of their owners' assets.

Human sacrifice Absent. Forbidden by most prevalent cults.

Religion

Majority religious practices Zoroastrianism; Nestorian Christianity; Manichaeism; Mahayana Buddhism.

China: Tang dynasty

Founded when the Duke of Tang, Li Yuan, seized the Sui capital of
Luoyang in 618 CE, the Tang dynasty, famed for its literature and
cosmopolitan culture, is widely considered a highpoint of imperial
China. The Tang conquered territory in Central Asia and northern
Korea. In 660 CE, Empress Wu became the first woman to rule China,
governing as regent and then empress dowager until her death in
705 CE. Declining authority in the 8th century CE culminated in the
rebellion of An Lushan, a Turkic general, who attempted to establish a new dynasty between 755 and 763 CE. The Tang government
remained nominally intact, but the empire slowly fractured over
the next century.

General
Duration 627–907 CE
Language Chinese (Sino-Tibetan)
Preceded by Sui dynasty
Succeeded by Five Dynasties and Ten Kingdoms period

Territory
Total area (km²) 6m in 627 CE; 5m in 700; 3.2m in 800; 1.6m in 900

People
Population 37m in 700 CE; 52m in 750
Largest city 1m (Chang'an)
Standing army 490,000–600,000

Social scale
Settlement hierarchy 1. Capital (Chang'an); 2. Large centres;

3. Medium-sized centres; 4. Small centres; 5. Villages;
6. Hamlets.

Administrative hierarchy 1. Emperor; 2. Central administration;
3. Prefects; 4. Prefectural administration; 5. County governors;
6. District officials; 7. Village elders.

Institutions

Legal code Emperor Gaozu (566–635 CE) commissioned creation of simpler, less harsh legal code.

Bureaucracy Professional. Three chief ministers supervised the Imperial Chancellery, Imperial Secretariat and the Department for State Affairs.

Religious validation of rule Mandate of Heaven

Property rights The imperial state in principle held claim to all land, though in practice large estates were controlled by Buddhist monasteries and private landowners.

Price controls Unclear

Banking regulations Probably present. Tang state maintained an early form of banking system from Chang'an after 700 CE.

Economy

Taxation Taxes on land; poll tax; state gained much revenue from the monopoly on salt production.

Coinage Present

Credit Banking services provided by Buddhist monasteries.

Agricultural practices

Main crops Millet. Wheat and rice also cultivated.

Irrigation Present

Fertilising Present

Cropping system Crop rotation

Metallurgy
Base metals Bronze, iron and steel

Military equipment
Handheld weapons War clubs, battle axes, daggers, swords, spears or
    lances, and halberds.
Armour Helmets, shields, breastplates, limb protection, chain mail,
    scale and lamellar coats.
Projectiles Composite bows and crossbows
Incendiaries Huoqiang: bamboo tube that could be filled with
    gunpowder and project flames/shoot projectiles.
Long walls Made use of pre-existing parts of the Great Wall.

Well-being
Life expectancy <30 years from birth
Average adult stature No data
Irrigation & drinking water New irrigation works established; canals
    diverted into reservoirs for drinking water.
Health care Both state and temple hospitals were staffed with
    trained physicians.
Alimentary support Some. Largely provided by Buddhist monasteries;
    state also provided some services.
Famine relief Granaries opened in response to natural disasters and
    were used to regulate the price of food to prevent price-related
    famine.

(In)equalities
Social mobility Examination system opened administrative roles to
    men theoretically from any background.
Occupational mobility Examination system opened administrative
    roles to men theoretically from any background.
Gender equality Official ideologies fostered gender inequality.
Slavery Present. Mostly employed in Buddhist monasteries.

Human sacrifice Absent. Forbidden by official ideologies.

Religion

Majority religious practices Confucianism (prevalent among state officials); Mahayana Buddhism (monasteries controlled money market and owned much land); Buddhists persecuted later in this period. Daoism (private religion of imperial family); Chinese folk religion (traditional practices still observed by large numbers of the population).

Iraq: Abbasid caliphate

The Abbasid dynasty, one the largest and powerful in the medieval Islamic world, began when Abu al-'Abbas al-Saffah led a revolt against Umayyad rule. The Abbasids derived their spiritual authority from their leadership of Sunni Islam, but made numerous provisions towards material concerns as well, maintaining public medical centres, public markets and libraries with drinking fountains. The reign of Harun al-Rashid (763–809 CE), whose rule is described in *The Thousand and One Nights*, is considered the dynasty's zenith, but by the end of the first millennium, the caliphs were figureheads, exerting little control over the regional powers that governed Abbasid territory.

General
Duration 750–946 CE; though Abbasid rule in name continued in Iraq
    until the mid-13th century.
Language Arabic (Afro-Asiatic)
Preceded by Umayyad caliphate
Succeeded by Buyid confederation

Territory
Total area (km²) 8.3m in 800 CE; 1m in 900 (core territory)

People
Population 23–33m in 800 CE; 9–11m in 900
Largest city 700,000 in 800 CE; 300,000–900,000 in 900 (Baghdad)
Standing army 100,000 in 762 CE

Social scale

Settlement hierarchy 1. Capital; 2. Large cities; 3. Provincial centres; 4. Provincial cities; 5. Towns; 6. Villages.

Administrative hierarchy 1. Caliph; 2. Wazir; 3. Central administration; 4. Governor of governors; 5. Governors; 6. District rulers; 7. City officials; 8. Village headman.

Institutions

Legal code Based on Islamic law.

Bureaucracy Professional

Religious validation of rule The caliph claimed God-given authority to implement Islamic law on earth.

Property rights Present

Price controls State imposed price controls on food during times of crisis.

Banking regulations Absent. No banking system in a modern sense.

Economy

Taxation Taxes on land, *jizya* (head tax on non-Muslims)

Coinage Gold *dinar*, silver *dirham* and *daniq* (1/6 of a *dinar* by weight), copper coins.

Credit A banking system centred in Baghdad enabled security-conscious travelling merchants to make cashless purchases.

Agricultural practices

Main crops Wheat and barley

Irrigation Present

Fertilising Present

Cropping system Fallowing, two-field rotation and nitrogen-fixing crops.

Metallurgy

Base metals Bronze, iron and steel

Military equipment

Handheld weapons Maces, pikes, broadswords, short swords and
daggers.

Armour Helmet, breastplate, coat of mail; wood and leather shield;
lamellar armour for limb protection; fireproof suit for naphtha
grenadiers.

Projectiles Javelins, composite bows, crossbows and slings

Incendiaries Greek fire and naphtha grenades

Long walls Inherited pre-existing defensive walls

Well-being

Life expectancy 35 years from birth

Average adult stature No data

Irrigation & drinking water New irrigation systems established
alongside new cities; water supply factored into the design of
cities.

Health care Mixed. Hospitals (*bimaristans*) provided free health-care
service; supported by private donations but also by the state.

Alimentary support *Zakat* (Islamic charity) and *jizya* (head tax on
non-Muslims) used to provide welfare for the poor, old,
orphaned, widowed and disabled.

Famine relief Food stored in case of famines.

(In)equalities

Social mobility Some. Worth noting that elite figures in the Abbasid
courts, caliphs included, were often descended from concubines
and/or enslaved people.

Occupational mobility Probably present

Gender equality Stark political, religious and legal distinctions based
on gender.

Slavery Slavery was widespread on farms, in homes and in craft industries; enslaved people were captured in wars or bought through trade.

Human sacrifice Absent. Forbidden by Islam.

Religion

Majority religious practices Sunni Islam; Shia Islam

France: Carolingian kingdom

In 752 CE, the Carolingians deposed the last Merovingian king, Childeric III, and seized outright control of Frankish territory. Carolingian kings maintained the decentralised Merovingian state apparatus, largely delegating power to militarised landowners. The empire expanded under Charlemagne, who claimed the Roman imperial title in 800 CE. The three sons of the second Carolingian king, Louis the Pious, vied for control of the empire on his death. The conflict was settled in 870 CE with the Treaty of Meerssen, which set a boundary that endures to the present day as the border between France and Germany. Western Frankish lands remained politically fragmented until 987 CE, when power passed to the Capetian dynasty.

General
Duration 752–987 CE
Languages Latin (Indo-European); Old French (Indo-European); Frankish (Indo-European).
Preceded by Merovingian kingdom
Succeeded by Capetian kingdom

Territory
Total area (km²) 1.1m in 752 CE; 2.2m in 850; 800,000 in 900; 675,000 in 950.

People
Population 7–9m in 800 CE; 4–5m in 900
Largest city 20,000 (Paris)

Standing army 10,000 professional core army; all free men could be
called up in an emergency.

Social scale

Settlement hierarchy 1. Large cities; 2. Towns; 3. Villages.

Administrative hierarchy 1. King; 2. Royal household, 3. Counts and
bishops; 4. Local administrators (eg *scabini,* viscounts).

Institutions

Legal code Absent. King's word was law, inscribed in legal texts
known as capitularies.

Bureaucracy Bureaucracy. Small number of court bureaucrats
(members of the royal household), including chancellor,
seneschal, butler, chamberlain and constable.

Religious validation of rule King crowned by pope, though on
principle of heredity; seen as supported by and representative of
God on earth.

Property rights Mixed. King owned all land, but his vassals had
rights of usufruct over their allocated portions of land.

Price controls Officially authorised royal markets and fairs increased
state revenue; participating merchants were subject to price
controls.

Banking regulations Absent. No banking due to state legislation
against usury.

Economy

Taxation Poorly developed; systematic taxation emerged much later.

Coinage 240 silver pence equalled one pound of silver.

Credit Absent. Rulers issued secular legislation banning anything
considered to be "usury".

Agricultural practices

Main crops Wheat, barley and oats

Irrigation Present

Fertilising Present

Cropping system Three-field rotation and nitrogen-fixing crops

Metallurgy

Base metals Bronze, iron and steel

Military equipment

Handheld weapons Most soldiers carried an iron-headed lance; kings and nobles carried swords.

Armour Helmets, shields and coats of mail

Projectiles Simple bows, composite bows and crossbows

Incendiaries Burning pitch and grease used in sieges

Long walls Absent

Well-being

Life expectancy 35 years from birth

Average adult stature 171 cm (male); 157 cm (female)

Irrigation & drinking water Absent. Small-scale irrigation only, some of it managed by the church; drinking water from rivers, wells and cisterns.

Health care Absent. Only provided by the church, and only towards the end of the period.

Alimentary support Charlemagne founded many hospices, which provided food and shelter for pilgrims and the needy; the church was also a source of support.

Famine relief Mixed. Usually provided by the church; special decrees issued to provide support in particularly dire emergencies.

(In)equalities

Social mobility Hereditary elite

Occupational mobility Largely absent. Highly hierarchical society;

occupational mobility mostly reserved for ethnic minorities and foreigners enjoying royal protection.

Gender equality Though not generally considered equal to men, women were permitted a number of roles within the church, and aristocratic women often managed estates or convents.

Slavery Estate records suggest that 10% of workers were enslaved.

Human sacrifice Absent. Forbidden by Christianity.

Religion

Majority religious practice Roman Catholicism

Japan: Heian period

Japan's Heian period began when Emperor Kammu moved the court from Nara to Heian (present-day Kyoto). Heian rulers controlled much of southern and central Japan, overseeing a vast bureaucracy. Over time, the imperial family became distant from the realities of government, occupying themselves with elaborate ceremonies and matters of protocol. While arts and culture flourished, lack of imperial engagement in the running of the state allowed the provincial warrior class to establish something close to feudal control. This laid the foundation for the *shogunate* – the military government which dominated Japan until the 1800s and left emperors as little more than figureheads.

General
Duration 794–1185 CE
Language Early Middle Japanese (Japonic)
Preceded by Nara period (Japan)
Succeeded by Kamakura Shogunate

Territory
Total area (km²) 250,000–300,000

People
Population 4m in 800 CE; 4.4–5.6m in 900; 4.5–5m in 1000; 5.5–6.3m in 1100.
Largest city 150,000 (Kyoto)
Standing army No data

Social scale

Settlement hierarchy 1. Capital (Kyoto); 2. Cities; 3. Town; 4. Villages.

Administrative hierarchy 1. Emperors; 2. Central Councils;
3. Ministers; 4. Lesser officials; 5. Provincial governors;
6. District governors; 7. Lesser administrators.

Institutions

Legal code *Yoro ritsuryo* code, promulgated in 757 CE.

Bureaucracy Professional. Bureaucrats came from the aristocracy,
but still received salaries.

Religious validation of rule Emperor was considered divine.

Property rights Aristocracy could own land.

Price controls After 841 CE the state copied the Chinese granary
system to manage the fluctuating prices of grain.

Banking regulations No data

Economy

Taxation Taxes on land; handicraft and *corvée* labour taxes based on
the number of adult males in an area.

Coinage Eight different coinages introduced throughout Heian era.

Credit State (as well as Buddhist temples and wealthy individuals)
loaned money or rice at specific rates of interest; letter of
exchange also known.

Agricultural practices

Main crops Rice. Barley also cultivated.

Irrigation Present

Fertilising Present

Cropping system Two-field rotation

Metallurgy

Base metals Bronze, iron and steel

Military equipment

Handheld weapons *Kanabou* (iron war club), curved swords, daggers, *yari* (spear) and *naginata* (polearm).

Armour Helmets, breastplates, scale and plate armour, and self-standing wooden shields.

Projectiles Simple bows, composite bows and crossbows

Incendiaries Fire arrows used in sieges.

Long walls Absent

Well-being

Life expectancy 40 years from birth

Average adult stature No data

Irrigation & drinking water Pre-existing irrigation systems used; wells; canals.

Health care Absent. Largely provided by private charitable institutions.

Alimentary support Governments made rice loans in time of famine; also provided by private charitable institutions.

Famine relief The state rice loan system and granary system designed to manage fluctuating prices may have softened the impact of the 860s famines.

(In)equalities

Social mobility Hereditary elite

Occupational mobility Limited

Gender equality Genders in many ways segregated; men allowed multiple wives but not vice versa.

Slavery Enslaved people were war captives, descendants of war captives, criminals, children sold into slavery, and debtors.

Human sacrifice Absent. Forbidden by Buddhism.

Religion

Majority religious practices Shinto; Mahayana Buddhism

Cambodia: Angkor kingdom

The Angkor kingdom (also known as the Khmer Empire) occupied an important position in the trade of rice, honey, spices, cloth and gold travelling to and from China to the north and India to the west. Contemporary visitors reported gold- and copper-capped temples, sumptuous religious festivals and a lively trade in Chinese goods; along with thousands of enslaved workers and servants. The ruler was known as *devaraja* (god-king) and patronised both Hinduism and Buddhism. Suryavarman II erected Angkor Wat, one of the largest religious structures in the world, dedicated to the Hindu god Vishnu. Attacks in the 1400s by the Ayutthaya peoples from Thailand forced Angkor nobles to flee, leaving most of the kingdom to Thai rulers.

General
Duration 800–1432 CE
Languages Khmer (Austroasiatic); Mon (Austroasiatic)
Preceded by Zhenla kingdom
Succeeded by Khmer kingdom of Cambodia

Territory
Total area (km²) 950,000

People
Population 1.5m
Largest city >750,000–1m (Angkor)
Standing army 20,000

Social scale

Settlement hierarchy 1. Capital (Angkor); 2. Large administrative
centres and former capitals; 3. Regional centres; 4. Village
centres; 5. Hamlets.

Administrative hierarchy 1. King (Raja); 2. Regional governors;
3. Provincial governors (*visayas*); 4. Settlement officials;
(*maichiechs*); 5. Village elders (*gramavrddhas*).

Institutions

Legal code Based on Hindu law.

Bureaucracy State maintained 2,740 administrative officials.

Religious validation of rule King was believed to be a god.

Property rights Present

Price controls Absent

Banking regulations No data

Economy

Taxation Taxes on land, property, trade, production and possibly
people.

Coinage Absent. The Khmer Empire never developed a standardised
currency, instead using exchange equivalents in gold, silver, rice,
cloth and cattle.

Credit Unclear. Chinese source says that women managed money-
changing and trade, so may also have issued credit.

Agricultural practices

Main crop Rice

Irrigation Present

Fertilising Absent

Cropping system Unclear

Metallurgy

Base metals Bronze and iron

Military equipment

Handheld weapons Knives, daggers, spears, lances, axes (*phkn'h*), sabres and broadswords.

Armour Armour made out of buffalo skin, tree bark, rattan cane, cloth or metals; helmets and shields; an inscription mentions a king clad in a coat of mail.

Projectiles Simple bows and crossbows

Incendiaries No evidence

Long walls No evidence

Well-being

Life expectancy No data

Average adult stature No data

Irrigation & drinking water Dams and reservoirs; irrigation network that grew to span 1,000 km^2.

Health care Present. For instance, King Jayavarman VII (r. 1181–1218 CE) boasted of establishing over one hundred hospitals.

Alimentary support Probably present. Probably provided by state-supported temples.

Famine relief Probably present. Probably provided by state-supported temples.

(In)equalities

Social mobility Hereditary elite

Occupational mobility Limited. Reserved for elites

Gender equality Women played important roles in temples and commerce; claimants to the throne could appeal to the female line; some elite women were literate.

Slavery Enslaved people made up a third of the population.

Human sacrifice Unclear. Some prisoners subjected to ritualised execution.

Religion

Majority religious practices Saivite Hinduism; Mahayana Buddhism

Italy: Medieval Papal States

The term "Papal States" was not adopted until around 1200 CE; at this time the polity of the papacy at Rome was called the Patrimony of Saint Peter, Republic of Saint Peter or Land of Saint Peter. Central Italy languished in many ways during this period, which was marked by a high degree of fragmentation and sub-regional autonomy. Various areas of the Patrimony of St Peter were virtually independent of the papacy or subject to central authority but in a nominal way. Beginning with Innocent III, though, the papacy extended its power over its various holdings, and over the other Christian kingdoms throughout western Europe. The period ends with the papal exile to Avignon in 1309 as a result of conflict with Philip IV of the French Capetian kingdom.

General
Duration 904–1309 CE
Language Latin (Indo-European)
Preceded by Republic of Saint Peter
Succeeded by Avignon papacy

Territory
Total area (km²) 14,000 in 1000 CE; 6,000 in 1100; 44,000 in 1200

People
Population 300,000–1.5m
Largest city 35,000 (Rome)
Standing army Unclear. Most armies fighting for or with the papacy were foreign; medieval chronicler Matteo Villani wrote that

Rome could field 20,000 men, but this was most probably a guess.

Social scale
Settlement hierarchy 1. Capital (Rome); 2. Cities with bishops; 3. Towns; 4. Nucleated village (*castelli, castra*).
Administrative hierarchy 1. Pope; 2. Major administrative officials; 3. Sub-division heads; 4. Duchy governors; 5. Bishops; 6. Rectors of the patrimony; 7. Village leaders.

Institutions
Legal code Mixed. Uniform code of law only introduced in 1357; before then, law rested on *Codex Justinianus*, canon law, papal bulls and the various constitutions and edicts that governed individual territories' relationship with the papacy.
Bureaucracy Mixed. Most major offices covered by high-ranking members of the clergy; closest thing to a secular administration were notaries, archivists and scribes attached to the central government.
Religious validation of rule Popes claimed to be the legitimate successors of Christ's first apostle, Peter.
Property rights Ownership of land could take many forms (individual, communal, institutional, kin-based, feudal, etc.).
Price controls In the cities, *Abbondanza* administrators regulated market prices for food.
Banking regulations Popes discouraged money-lending generally and enacted a number of measures specifically meant to hinder the lending activities of the society's Jewish minority.

Economy
Taxation Present
Coinage Papal currency initially imitated the *denier* of the

Champagne region in France; another coin called the *grosso* was introduced in the 1250s CE.

Credit In spite of attempts to curtail usury, many banking houses existed for loans and credit; the *instrumentum ex causa cambii*, introduced in the 13th century CE, allowed borrowers to receive credit in their local currency as long as they promised to pay later in another.

Agricultural practices
Main crops Wheat, olives and grapes
Irrigation Present
Fertilising Present
Cropping system Crop rotation and nitrogen-fixing crops

Metallurgy
Base metals Bronze, iron and steel

Military equipment
Handheld weapons Battle axes, swords, spears and lances
Armour Helmets, shields, leather and quilted armour, metal breastplates, limb protection and chain mail.
Projectiles Bows and crossbows
Incendiaries May have been used by mercenaries.
Long walls Absent

Well-being
Life expectancy No data
Average adult stature No data
Irrigation & drinking water Agrarian development in the Roman hinterland took off in 1050–1100 CE; restoration and maintenance of Roman aqueducts started in the late 8th/early 9th centuries CE.

Health care A very large hospital, the first on its scale in Europe, the Santo Spirito, was founded in Rome by Innocent III in 1198 CE.

Alimentary support Santo Spirito hospital provided food and clothing for the poor and cared for orphans; help was also available in rural and urban locations at a building known by the Byzantine Greek term *xenodocheia*.

Famine relief Abbondanza magistracies managed the market price of food to keep it affordable and used stockpiled grain reserves to subsidise prices whenever it became necessary.

(In)equalities

Social mobility Mixed. Noble families and nepotism dominated the papal government, but in rare cases foreigners, church officials with no church background and commoners were not excluded and could reach high positions (Innocent IV was from a wealthy merchant family; the father of Urban IV was a cobbler).

Occupational mobility Limited. Urban growth encouraged occupational diversification, but craft and merchant guilds in towns made it more difficult for outsiders and people from non-professional or artisanal families to enter into the business.

Gender equality The role of women in public life was almost entirely channelled through membership of monasteries and religious orders, where they engaged in ritual, commercial and charitable activities.

Slavery Church maintained an ambivalent stance towards slavery, which it only officially abolished in its territories in 1831.

Human sacrifice Absent. Forbidden by Christianity.

Religion

Majority religious practice Roman Catholicism

Iceland: Icelandic Commonwealth

Settlers from Norway and Norse colonies in Scotland and Ireland began arriving in Iceland in significant numbers in the late 9th century CE. The Icelandic Commonwealth began in 930 CE. At this time, Icelandic society was a federation of small, rural communities in relatively small, scattered settlements. Initially pagan, the adoption of Christianity brought Iceland wealth and cultural knowledge through the efforts of bishops, monks and wealthy lords of continental European ancestry, and helped to produce numerous sagas: semi-mythic tales written in Icelandic using the Latin alphabet. Competition between independent lords eventually led to civil warfare, which ended when local lords swore allegiance to the Norwegian crown.

General
Duration 930–1262 CE
Language Old Norse (Indo-European)
Preceded by Norse Settler period
Succeeded by Kingdom of Norway

Territory
Total area (km²) 103,000 (size of Iceland)

People
Population 10,000 in 930 CE; 31,000 in 1100; 50,000–60,000 in 1262
Largest city 200–300. No true cities; this is a rough figure for a typical larger settlement.
Standing army 500–1,000 (private armies)

Social scale

Settlement hierarchy 1. Bishoprics and elite residences; 2. Manor farms; 3. Homesteads.

Administrative hierarchy 1. Commonwealth Assembly; 2. Local assemblies or territorial lordships; 3. Chieftains or communes (*hreppar*)

Institutions

Legal code Based on Norwegian law, brought to Iceland with the early settlers; not written down.

Bureaucracy Absent

Religious validation of rule Chieftains claimed divine descent; after conversion, important to demonstrate the church's blessing.

Property rights Present

Price controls Absent

Banking regulations Absent

Economy

Taxation Absent. No tax collected by a centralised state; farmers paid taxes to chiefs; church able to raise funds with Tithe Law of 1096 CE.

Coinage Absent

Credit Unclear

Agricultural practices

Main crop Animal products (dairy)

Irrigation Unclear

Fertilising Probably present

Cropping system Animal husbandry. Some crop rotation may have been employed, but sources are unclear.

Metallurgy

Base metals Bronze, iron and steel

Military equipment

Handheld weapons Battle axes, swords, daggers, spears and polearms

Armour Chain mail, helmets and shields

Projectiles Javelins and simple bows; likely that slings and perhaps
    composite bows existed but were not commonly used;
    crossbows present in 12th century CE.

Incendiaries Not known to have been used.

Long walls Not known to have been built.

Well-being

Life expectancy No data

Average adult stature 170 cm (male)

Irrigation & drinking water Absent. Dams, canals and drinking wells
    existed, but they were built by private parties.

Health care Absent. Some services provided by monasteries.

Alimentary support Absent. Some services provided by monasteries.

Famine relief Unclear. Some services provided by monasteries;
    hreppar had communal granaries.

(In)equalities

Social mobility Hereditary elite

Occupational mobility Limited

Gender equality Men and women had different legal rights.

Slavery Present 930–1096 CE (chattel slavery and debt slavery);
    absent 1096–1262 (forbidden by Christianity).

Human sacrifice Present 930–1096 CE (during crises); absent
    1096–1262 (forbidden by Christianity).

Religion

Majority religious practices Nordic religion 930–1096 CE; Roman
    Catholicism 1096–1262.

USA: Cahokia settlement, Lohmann-Stirling period

Cahokia was a large and complex pre-contact society situated on the banks of the Mississippi. It began around 1000 CE with a sudden – and still unexplained – influx of people into the previously sparsely populated river valley. The new arrivals brought distinctive social and settlement structures, including grand mounds. At its zenith, there were at least 50,000 people living in the 2,000 km² region surrounding the central mound. The Cahokians of this time are renowned for the construction of monumental works such as the famous Monks Mound, which required moving 1.1 million m³ of earth, as well as a 15 m-high wooden palisade that ran for nearly 3 km.

General
Duration 1050–1199 CE
Language Siouan (unclear); generally held (but difficult to prove)
   belief is that they were Siouan speakers, probably Dhegihan.
Preceded by Emergent Mississippian period
Succeeded by Cahokia, Moorehead period

Territory
Total area (km²) 2,000–3,000 (extent of core region)

People
Population 40,000–50,000
Largest city 10,000–15,000 (Cahokia)
Standing army No data

Social scale
Settlement hierarchy 1. Central administrative complex (Cahokia);

2. Mound complexes near Cahokia; 3. Possible centres of
subordinate societies; 4. Smaller settlements.

Administrative hierarchy 1. Supreme Priest-Chief; 2. Lesser priest-
chiefs; 3. Elders/kin-group leaders.

Institutions
Legal code No data

Bureaucracy Probably absent

Religious validation of rule Probably derived from performance of
ritual.

Property rights Unclear. Suggested, perhaps, by proliferation of
single-family farmsteads in peripheral areas.

Price controls Probably absent

Banking regulations Probably absent

Economy
Taxation Probably absent

Coinage Absent

Credit No data

Agricultural practices
Main crop Maize

Irrigation Absent

Fertilising Present

Cropping system Two-field rotation and nitrogen-fixing crops

Metallurgy
Base metals Absent

Military equipment
Handheld weapons Stone maces, stone axes and war clubs; possibly
other weapons made of wood.

Armour No evidence, but could be because armour was made out of perishable materials, eg wood.

Projectiles Simple bows and thrown spears

Incendiaries No evidence

Long walls No evidence

Well-being

Life expectancy Average age at death: 40 years (male); 35 years (female)

Average adult stature No data

Irrigation & drinking water Probably absent

Health care No data

Alimentary support Probably present. Communal storehouses are known from the archaeological record; food distributed at festivals.

Famine relief No data

(In)equalities

Social mobility Hereditary elite

Occupational mobility Probably absent. Highly hierarchical society; limited evidence of occupational diversity.

Gender equality Archaeologists have discovered the remains of at least two mass sacrifices of young women.

Slavery Probably present. May be inferred from sacrifice of retainers during funerary ceremonies for elite men.

Human sacrifice Retainers sacrificed as part of funerary ceremonies for elite men.

Religion

Majority religious practice Mississippian religion. Archaeological evidence for large-scale burial and/or feasting rituals, centring around mound structures.

Colombia: Tairona

Tairona generally refers to indigenous groups of the Sierra Nevada de Santa Marta – a mountain range stretching along Colombia's Caribbean coast. At the time of the Spanish Conquest in 1524 CE, the Tairona were organised into semi-independent villages governed by a priestly class and a hierarchy of chiefs. Ecological diversity in the region allowed for intensive agricultural production, supporting a thriving economy in north Colombia at the time. Tairona villages included workshops for craft specialists (gold smelters, semi-precious stone engravers and merchants) along with large ceremonial complexes, some of which were used for feasting. These villages supported cultural diversity as well, especially with regards to religion and language.

General
Duration 1050–1524 CE
Language Atanque (Chibcha)
Preceded by Neguanje phase
Succeeded by Habsburg Spanish Empire

Territory
Total area (km²) 150 (typical size of an independent community)

People
Population 1,000–3,000 (typical population of an independent community).
Largest city 100–200 in 1100 CE; 150–4,000 in 1150–1399; 3,000–5,000 in 1400–1524 (Pueblito).

Standing army No data

Social scale

Settlement hierarchy 1. Major centres; 2. Large towns; 3. Pueblos (villages).

Administrative hierarchy 1. High priest (*naoma*); 2. Chiefly overlord; 3. Chief (*cacique*); 4. Sub-chief.

Institutions

Legal code Probably absent

Bureaucracy Probably absent

Religious validation of rule No data

Property rights No data

Price controls Probably absent

Banking regulations Probably absent

Economy

Taxation No data

Coinage Absent

Credit Probably absent

Agricultural practices

Main crop Maize

Irrigation Present

Fertilising Present

Cropping system Swidden farming, gradually replaced by fertilised farming.

Metallurgy

Base metal Copper

Military equipment

Handheld weapons War clubs and maces

Armour No data

Projectiles Simple bows and darts
Incendiaries Fire arrows
Long walls Probably absent

Well-being
Life expectancy No data
Average adult stature No data
Irrigation & drinking water Irrigation canals and terraces
Health care No data
Alimentary support No data
Famine relief No data

(In)equalities
Social mobility Hereditary elite
Occupational mobility No data
Gender equality Probably absent
Slavery No data
Human sacrifice Probably absent. No archaeological evidence and
    not mentioned in Spanish accounts.

Religion
Majority religious practice Tairona religion. Probably involved
    shamanic practices and animistic beliefs.

Mongolia: Mongolian Empire

The product of a series of remarkable campaigns across Eurasia over the 13th century CE, the Mongolian Empire was history's largest land empire. The Mongols were just one of many nomadic tribes living on the Central Asian Steppe, until a man named Temujin or Temuchin (later called Chinggis) became Khan at the end of the 12th century. Chinggis united the tribes into an empire which conquered Russia and parts of north China, demolished the Abbasid caliphate, and took Germanic territory in eastern Europe. The Mongols stopped short of conquering the divided Christian kingdoms of western Europe, but historians generally agree they could have if they had wished.

General
Duration 1206–71 CE
Language Mongolian (Mongolic)
Preceded by Early Mongol confederacy
Succeeded by Yuan dynasty and various khanates

Territory
Total area (km²) 25m (at its greatest extent)

People
Population 70m (at its greatest)
Largest city 600,000–800,000 (Hangzhou)
Standing army 100,000–200,000

Social scale
Settlement hierarchy 1. Capital; 2. Regional centres; 3. Cities;
    4. Towns; 5. Villages; 6. Nomadic camps.

Administrative hierarchy 1. Khan; 2. Royal household; 3. Dependent and tributary rulers; 4. Provincial governors; 5. Local administrators.

Institutions

Legal code Probably absent. Scholars have recently disputed the existence of a Mongol law code ("Great Yasa").

Bureaucracy Probably absent. The Mongol state included several administrative roles, but they were probably non-specialists recruited from the military elite.

Religious validation of rule Great Khan believed to enact the will of Möngke Tengri (Everlasting Heaven).

Property rights Relative to land and livestock

Price controls Probably absent

Banking regulations Probably absent

Economy

Taxation Taxes imposed on farmers.

Coinage Currencies previously in use in conquered territories remained in use.

Credit Credit systems previously in place in conquered territories remained in use.

Agricultural practices

Main crops None in core territory; a variety of crops (including wheat, rice and millet) were grown in conquered territories.

Irrigation Mixed

Fertilising Mixed

Cropping system Animal husbandry and seasonal harvesting. Cropping system in conquered territories remained in use.

Metallurgy

Base metals Bronze, iron and steel

Military equipment

Handheld weapons Hooked spears used against cavalry, lances, sabres, daggers, axes and maces.

Armour Wooden shields, leather and steel helmets, layered hide body armour, chain mail to cover the neck, some use of scale and possibly lamellar body armour.

Projectiles Javelins, composite bows and crossbows

Incendiaries Naphtha and grenades

Long walls Not known to have been built.

Well-being

Life expectancy 25 years from birth

Average adult stature No data

Irrigation & drinking water Water supply systems previously in place in conquered territories remained in use, with the exception of the Central Asian irrigation networks.

Health care Sporadic. Not directly provided by the Mongol state, but by local authorities.

Alimentary support Sporadic. Not directly provided by the Mongol state, but by local authorities.

Famine relief Sporadic. Not directly provided by the Mongol state, but by local authorities.

(In)equalities

Social mobility Hereditary elite

Occupational mobility Mixed. Differed depending on the region.

Gender equality Mongol society was patriarchal and patrilineal, but some elite women were able to exercise great influence, and two became empress regents in the 1240s; little is known about commoner women.

Slavery War captives often enslaved.

Human sacrifice Performed at coronations and funerals of leaders, and when war mobilised.

Religion
Majority religious practices Mongolian Shamanism; Tengriism. Other faiths practised by conquered populations.

Egypt: Mamluk sultanate

The Mamluks wrested power from the Ayyubid caliphate, taking control over much of the Levant along with Egypt and parts of the Arab peninsula. Mamluk is an Arabic term used to designate the class of highly trained enslaved people mobilised by medieval Islamic rulers for military and administrative duties. The Mamluks oversaw an era of prosperity in Egypt, which peaked under the reign of Sultan Nasiri. However, prosperity was brought to an end by the Black Death, which arrived in Alexandria in 1347 CE. Mamluk law prevented the children of mamluks from becoming mamluks – a means of thwarting nepotism and corruption. Consequently, the ruling elite had to be constantly replaced by new "slave" recruits taken mainly from Crimea and the Caucasus.

General
Duration 1260–1517 CE
Language Arabic (Afro-Asiatic)
Preceded by Ayyubid sultanate
Succeeded by Ottoman Empire

Territory
Total area (km²) 2.1m

People
Population 6–7m in 1300 CE; 4.8m in 1400; 6m in 1500
Largest city 200,000 in 1300 CE; 150,000–350,000 in 1400; 150,000–400,000 in 1500 (Cairo).
Standing army 40,000–50,000

Mali: Mali Empire

In the early 13th century, several Malinke chiefdoms from the upper Niger Delta region united against the Sosso kingdom, forming the Mali Empire, the largest of the medieval West African empires. Under Musa I ("Mansa Musa") the Mali Empire controlled over 24 cities and their surrounding territories, bounded by the Atlantic, the Niger Inland Delta, the Sahara and the tropical forest belt. Mansa Musa is famed for his patronage of Islam and his lavish distribution of gold while on pilgrimage to Mecca in 1325 CE. The cities of Mali were cosmopolitan, exporting gold, ivory, salt and enslaved people across the Sahara. Their characteristic mud-brick architecture, known as *banco*, can still be admired today.

General
Duration 1230–1410 CE
Languages Mande (Afro-Asiatic), Arabic (Afro-Asiatic)
Preceded by Sosso kingdom
Succeeded by Mande states

Territory
Total area (km²) >1.5m

People
Population 4–5m
Largest city 12,000–17,000 (based on evidence that medium-sized towns had 10,000–15,000 inhabitants).
Standing army 8,700 (size of King Mansa Musa's military escort in his famed pilgrimage to Mecca).

Social scale

Settlement hierarchy 1. Capital; 2. Market towns; 3. Mud-walled towns (*kafu*); 4. Villages.

Administrative hierarchy 1. King; 2. Court administrators; 3. Regional governors; 4. Village headmen.

Institutions

Legal code Mixed. Customary law prevailed but significant Muslim minority followed Islamic law.

Bureaucracy Limited. Court administrators known to have existed but very little else known about them.

Religious validation of rule Unclear 1230–1310 CE; divine support after Islamic conversion 1311–1410.

Property rights Unclear. Cultural understanding that anyone could have their own patch of land; sale of land not common practice.

Price controls No data

Banking regulations Probably present

Economy

Taxation Taxes on land, trade and production.

Coinage Unclear. Evidence of local manufacture of unstamped gold disks (*sola*).

Credit Loans were issued and debts were acknowledged in writing.

Agricultural practices

Main crop Rice

Irrigation Absent

Fertilising Absent

Cropping system A mixture of short-fallow and shifting cultivation

Metallurgy

Base metals Bronze, iron and perhaps steel

Military equipment

Handheld weapons Swords, spears and lances

Armour Mail coats, breastplates, shields, helmets and limb protection; largely reserved for nobles.

Projectiles Javelins and simple bows

Incendiaries No evidence

Long walls No long walls known to have been built.

Well-being

Life expectancy No data

Average adult stature No data

Irrigation & drinking water Probably present

Health care No data

Alimentary support No data

Famine relief No data

(In)equalities

Social mobility Probably absent

Occupational mobility Probably absent

Gender equality Unclear, but worth noting that the Manden or Kurukan Fuga Charter, a sort of oral "constitution" for the Mali Empire, gave equal rights to men and women.

Slavery Probably present. Chattel slavery; war captives usually enslaved.

Human sacrifice Probably absent. No clear evidence that it was practised; as Islamic beliefs spread, they would have included prohibition against human sacrifice.

Religion

Majority religious practices Mali religion; Sufi Islam

Social scale

Settlement hierarchy 1. Capital (Cairo); 2. Provincial capitals (eg Damascus); 3. Ritual or economic centres (eg Mecca, Alexandria); 4. Towns; 5. Villages; 6. Hamlets.

Administrative hierarchy 1. Sultan; 2. Central administrators; 3. Provincial governors; 4. District governor; 5. Town governor; 6. Lesser officials.

Institutions

Legal code Based on Islamic law.

Bureaucracy Professional. Recruited from the ranks of enslaved people.

Religious validation of rule Sultans responsible for promoting Islamic ideals. A sultan had to have been a manumitted Mamluk slave.

Property rights Present

Price controls Some. Attempted in times of famine; there was a market inspector (*muhtasib*); in times of plenty, officials withheld supplies from large grain stores to raise market price.

Banking regulations Absent. No established banking system due to the Islamic prohibition against interest.

Economy

Taxation Taxes on land, trade and agricultural produce

Coinage Gold *dinars*, silver *dirhams*. In the 15th century CE, an unskilled labourer could expect a month's wage of just over 3 *dinars*; however, there was considerable fluctuation in the value of currency through the centuries.

Credit The Karimi merchant family loaned money to the government; the sultan's public granaries loaned seed and food.

Agricultural practices

Main crops Wheat and barley

Irrigation Present

Fertilising Present

Cropping system Nutrient replacement of soil with annual flooding

Metallurgy

Base metals Bronze, iron and steel

Military equipment

Handheld weapons Iron maces, battle axes, daggers, straight-bladed swords and spears.

Armour Wooden shields, leather helmets and cuirasses, chain mail and *qarqal* (a scale/lamellar coat).

Projectiles Composite bows and crossbows

Incendiaries Naphtha bombs and hand grenades

Long walls No evidence

Well-being

Life expectancy 30–35 years from birth

Average adult stature No data

Irrigation & drinking water New irrigation canals and dams built; public fountains in cities; extensive aqueduct in Cairo.

Health care Mixed. Sultan Qalawun (1279–90 CE) commissioned a large hospital complex with capacity for 4,000 patients; however, hospitals were usually in private hands.

Alimentary support Mixed. Public granaries loaned food; *waqf* foundations provided support for orphans.

Famine relief Public granaries loaned food; during the 1295–96 famine the sultan ordered the aristocracy to provide to those in need.

(In)equalities

Social mobility Limited. Positions of power reserved for Mamluks.

Occupational mobility Limited. Administrative roles reserved for

Mamluks; opportunities for occupational mobility in
commercial, religious and charitable fields for wealthier classes.

Gender equality Though not exactly considered equal to men, a wide
range of roles were open to elite women, including teacher, juror
and charitable donor.

Slavery Rulers and many senior officials were recruited from the
ranks of enslaved people.

Human sacrifice Absent. Forbidden by Islam.

Religion

Majority religious practices Sunni Islam; Sufi Islam

Indonesia: Majapahit Empire

Covering much of the eastern half of what is today the island of
Java, the Majapahit Empire claimed sovereignty over most of the
Indonesian archipelago and the Malay peninsula. The kingdom
marks Indonesia's transition to powerful, centralised states. The
imperial court dealt directly with local Hindu temple officials and
established trade links with the villages, often providing tax exemption to temple elites and loyal village elders. Majapahit gradually
succumbed to internal succession disputes and external attacks,
not least by the Chinese Ming dynasty. The Islamic Demak sultanate
ended the Majapahit, seizing vital sea trade routes in the early 16th
century and then east Java itself.

General
Duration 1292–1518 CE
Languages Middle Javanese (Austronesian); Sanskrit (Indo-European)
Preceded by Singhasari kingdom
Succeeded by Demak sultanate

Territory
Total area (km²) 500,000

People
Population 5m
Largest city 200,000 (Trowulan)
Standing army 30,000

Social scale
Settlement hierarchy 1. Capital (Trowulan); 2. Villages; 3. Hamlets.

Administrative hierarchy 1. King; 2. Royal council; 3. Council of
ministers; 4. Provincial governors; 5. State officials in charge of
villages.

Institutions

Legal code Present

Bureaucracy Court administrators existed.

Religious validation of rule King believed to be a god.

Property rights New charters allowed wealthy but landless families
to buy land.

Price controls No data

Banking regulations No data

Economy

Taxation Land tax assessed in weight of precious metal and paid in
kind once or twice a year (spring/autumn).

Coinage Chinese copper coinage used.

Credit No data

Agricultural practices

Main crop Rice

Irrigation Present

Fertilising Present

Cropping system Fertilising and irrigation farming; double-cropping
of rice; swidden farming practised in parts of Java as well.

Metallurgy

Metals Bronze, iron and perhaps steel

Military equipment

Handheld weapons War clubs, battle axes, daggers, swords, spears,
toyas (wooden staffs) and *tjabangs* (forked iron truncheons).

Armour Depicted in iconography, which is, however, difficult to
    interpret.
Projectiles Javelins and simple bows
Incendiaries No evidence
Long walls None

Well-being
Life expectancy No data
Average adult stature No data
Irrigation & drinking water Rulers encouraged irrigation projects with
    tax incentives; drinking water supply system in Trowulan.
Health care No state health care; elite had access to physicians,
    commoners to healers known as *janggan*.
Alimentary support Absent
Famine relief Absent

(In)equalities
Social mobility Hereditary elite
Occupational mobility Limited, despite absence of true caste system
Gender equality Despite generalised male dominance, women often
    held the important role of diplomatic negotiator.
Slavery Mostly debt slavery.
Human sacrifice Unclear. Debated by experts.

Religion
Majority religious practice Saivite Hinduism

India: Vijayanagara Empire

Named after the fortified city at its centre, the Vijayanagara Empire ruled most of the modern southern Indian states of Karnataka, Andhra Pradesh, Goa, Kerala and Tamil Nadu. Under Vijayanagara, the region flourished: Hindu temples and royal palaces were built, trade and agriculture boomed, new towns were founded and new legal rights emerged. Initially, Vijayanagara's kings were content to be conquerors, but Krishnadevaraya (r. 1509–29) began the practice of placing loyal brahmans and military commanders in high offices and extracting monetary tribute from lords. Civil wars coupled with invasions from the north led to collapse in the 17th century and most of the subcontinent fell under the aegis of the Mughal Empire.

General

Duration 1336–1646 CE

Languages Sanskrit (Indo-European); Telugu (Dravidian); Tamil (Dravidian); Kannada (Dravidian).

Preceded by Delhi sultanate

Succeeded by Mughal Empire

Territory

Total area (km²) 350,000–370,000

People

Population 25m

Largest city 100,000 in 1400 CE; 150,000–250,000 in 1500 (Vijayanagara).

Standing army 50,000–90,000

Social scale

Settlement hierarchy 1. Capital (Vijayanagara); 2. Provincial capital;
3. Towns; 4. Villages.

Administrative hierarchy 1. King; 2. Council of ministers; 3. Central
administration; 4. Viceroy; 5. Provincial administration;
6. Village administration.

Institutions

Legal code Based on Hindu law.

Bureaucracy Professional. Local administrators paid in land and
agricultural produce.

Religious validation of rule King consecrated by priestly caste
(Brahmans).

Property rights Unclear

Price controls No data

Banking regulations No data

Economy

Taxation Land tax; "professional tax" on non-agricultural
professions.

Coinage Mostly gold and copper coins, but silver was also produced.

Credit State gave small farmers fields to cultivate with loaned seed.

Agricultural practices

Main crops Rice, wheat, sorghum and pulses

Irrigation Present

Fertilising Present

Cropping system Nitrogen-fixing crops

Metallurgy

Base metals Bronze, iron and steel

Military equipment

Handheld weapons Swords, spears, daggers and battle axes

Armour Leather armour covered whole body; iron plates could be inserted for additional protection; shields; cavalry troopers wore headpieces shaped like helmets.

Projectiles Javelins, simple bows and muskets

Incendiaries Explosive weapons to defend forts; artillery

Long walls No evidence

Well-being

Life expectancy No data

Average adult stature No data

Irrigation & drinking water Present

Health care Mixed. No state health care; some services provided by *choultries*, charitable institutions supported by private donors.

Alimentary support Mixed. *Ramanujakutas* (pilgrim's feeding houses) were supported by private donors, and also by the king himself.

Famine relief Mixed. Indirectly, through the preventive construction of water tanks and canals for irrigation.

(In)equalities

Social mobility Limited. Caste system. Worth noting that merchants and artisans gained wealth and prestige at this time.

Occupational mobility Absent. Caste system.

Gender equality Though certain aspects of Hindu ideology promote certain forms of gender inequality, Portuguese accounts tell of female judges, bailiffs, palace sentinels, diviners, accountants and record-keepers.

Slavery Chattel slavery.

Human sacrifice Probably absent

Religion

Majority religious practice Hinduism

Russia: Sakha peoples

The Lena River Valley (also known as Yakutia) in eastern Siberia is over four times the size of Texas and is one of the coldest places on earth. The Sakha (or Yakut) people have lived there since at least the 13th century CE. Early communities existed as semi-nomadic groups, breeding cattle and horses, and alternating between winter yurts and summer homesteads. When the first Cossacks arrived in the 1620s, the Yakut received them with hospitality, but skirmishes followed, in which the Yakut were led by the legendary hero Tygyn. From 1642 until the Russian Revolution, the region fell under tribute to the Russian tsar. It was one of the last Russian territories consolidated under the Soviet regime.

General
Duration 1400–1632 CE
Language Yakut (Turkic)
Preceded by Kurumchi culture
Succeeded by Russian Empire

Territory
Total area (km²) No data. Clan systems could cover vast areas but these would not have been fixed.

People
Population 500–1000. Estimate of size of average tribal group.
Largest city <100. No cities, only temporary camps with no more than 100 inhabitants.
Standing army Absent

Social scale

Settlement hierarchy 1. Temporary camps

Administrative hierarchy 1. Kin-based councils

Institutions

Legal code Absent

Bureaucracy Absent

Religious validation of rule Leaders believed to be descended from gods.

Property rights Land, cattle and horses controlled by the patriline.

Price controls Absent

Banking regulations Absent

Economy

Taxation Absent

Coinage Absent

Credit Probably absent

Agricultural practices

Main crops None. Subsistence based on animal products.

Irrigation Absent

Fertilising Absent

Cropping system Animal husbandry

Metallurgy

Base metal Iron

Military equipment

Handheld weapons Battle axes, daggers and spears

Armour Protection for cavalry; coats of mail over leather; helmets, shields and breastplates.

Projectiles Javelins and bows

Incendiaries Not known to have been used.

Long walls No long walls known to have been built.

Well-being
Life expectancy No data
Average adult stature Unclear
Irrigation & drinking water Absent. Economy centred on pastoralism.
Health care Absent
Alimentary support Absent
Famine relief Absent

(In)equalities
Social mobility Absent
Occupational mobility Probably absent. Though no strong division of labour.
Gender equality Strict sexual division of labour based on gender: men looked after horses, hunted and worked with metal; women looked after cattle, and made clothes and pottery.
Slavery Chattel slavery; war captives usually enslaved.
Human sacrifice Retainer sacrifice at leaders' funerals.

Religion
Majority religious practice Yakut Shamanism

Peru: Inca Empire

The Incas ruled over the largest indigenous empire in the Americas, which they referred to as the *Tawantinsuyu* ("the four parts together") to denote its sheer vastness. They forcibly relocated subject populations, often into specialised enclaves, such as the weavers and potters of Milliraya. Elites deployed ideology to consolidate their rule, providing free maize-beer at state-sponsored feasts and in return for labour services, while in rare cases conducting human sacrifices in honour of deities and sacred places. Epidemics in the early 16th century – possibly smallpox introduced by European invaders – left the Incas divided and ultimately unable to fend off Spain's conquistadors, who eventually conquered nearly all their territory. Nevertheless, resistance persisted until Peruvian independence in 1821.

General
Duration 1375–1532 CE
Languages Quechua (Quechuan) and Aymara (Aymaran)
Preceded by Late Intermediate period (Peru)
Succeeded by Habsburg Spanish Empire

Territory
Total area (km²) 500,000–2m

People
Population 6–14m in 1532
Largest city 20,000–100,000 (Cuzco)
Standing army 100,000

Social scale

Settlement hierarchy 1. Capital (Cuzco); 2. Provincial centres;
    3. Towns; 4. Villages; 5. Hamlets.

Administrative hierarchy 1. Ruler (Sapa Inca); 2. Region (*suyu*)
    governors (*apus*); 3. Provincial governors (*tokrikoqs*); 4. District
    governors (*hunu kurakas*); 5. Lesser *kurakas*.

Institutions

Legal code Present (despite absence of writing system or a dedicated
    state-run court system). Much leeway given to local leaders to
    administer justice in their territories.

Bureaucracy Professional. Quipu specialists (*quipucamayocs*) kept
    records using knots on string; census takers; managers of postal
    stations.

Religious validation of rule The Sapa Inca ("Emperor") was considered
    superhuman with a strong connection to the supernatural.

Property rights No data

Price controls Absent

Banking regulations Absent. No banks.

Economy

Taxation Labour tax imposed on married males between the ages of
    about 25 and 50.

Coinage Absent

Credit Probably absent

Agricultural practices

Main crops Maize, quinoa and potatoes

Irrigation Present

Fertilising Present

Cropping system Crop rotation

Metallurgy
Base metal Bronze

Military equipment
Handheld weapons War clubs, battle axes, daggers, spears, and
wooden swords with serrated edges.
Armour Soldiers had leather shields, woven cane helmets and
copper breastplates; nobles wore jewel-studded armour and
chest and back plates made of gold and silver.
Projectiles Javelins, slings, simple bows and *atlatls*
Incendiaries No evidence
Long walls A number of defensive walls built by Manco Inca.

Well-being
Life expectancy No data
Average adult stature 159 cm (male); 146 cm (female)
Irrigation & drinking water Mixed. Irrigation present, but no large-
scale drinking water supply system known.
Health care No data. Physicians existed but no evidence for state
provision of health care.
Alimentary support Officials distributed food and drink at large
festivals but there is no evidence for the existence of a
centralised alimentary support system.
Famine relief State stores were opened during times of famine.

(In)equalities
Social mobility Hereditary elite
Occupational mobility Absent. Occupations hereditary and restricted
to class.
Gender equality Men and women guilty of same crimes punished
differently; public roles generally reserved for men, though men
and women served in important religious roles.
Slavery Unclear. Economy based on serfdom rather than slavery,

though some servants of elite households (*yanakuna*), often
taken as military prisoners, faced lifetime obligations that were
inherited by their children.

Human sacrifice Multiple forms practised; known victims were
mostly children, but some evidence that on rare occasions
prisoners of war and retainers were sacrificed as well.

Religion

Majority religious practice Inca religion. Centred on worship of Sapa
Inca and gods representing the sun, moon and other natural
entities.

Turkey: Ottoman Emirate

Not to be confused with the empire that was a major global power of the Early Modern period, the Ottoman Emirate began as a small Turkish principality bordering the Byzantine realm. Turkish and other groups from the Caucasus and Balkans launched nearly constant raids against the Byzantines. Through warfare and diplomacy, the Islamic Ottomans eventually forced the submission of the western Balkans. Capitalising on these gains, the Ottomans were able to expand their territory rapidly. The western march of the armies of Timur (also known as Tamerlane) and his Timurid Empire halted the Ottoman expansion, which culminated in their defeat and vassalage in 1402.

General

Duration 1299–1402 CE

Languages Turkish (Turkic); Arabic (Afro-Asiatic); Persian (Indo-European)

Preceded by Byzantine Empire; Karamanid Emirate

Succeeded by Timurid Empire

Territory

Total area (km²) 18,000 in 1320 CE; 690,000 in 1400

People

Population 200,000–300,000 in 1325 CE; 5m in 1400

Largest city 20,000–30,000 (Bursa)

Standing army 20,000 in 1350 CE; 85,000 in 1400

Social scale

Settlement hierarchy 1. Capital; 2. Provincial centres; 3. Towns;
4. Villages.

Administrative hierarchy 1290–1326 CE: 1. Sultan; 2. Central
administrators; 3. Provincial governors. 1326–60 CE: 1. Chief;
2. Council of Elders. 1360–1413 CE: 1. Sultan; 2. Imperial Council;
3. Chancellor; 4. Provincial governors; 5. District governors;
6. Judges in towns and cities.

Institutions

Legal code Introduced in 1325 CE.

Bureaucracy Absent

Religious validation of rule Sultan seen as warrior serving God and
carrying out divine instructions.

Property rights Mixed. Most land was state owned and allocated to
peasants for cultivation; however, in conquered territories, old
forms of property ownership were left in place.

Price controls Unclear. Price regulation common in later centuries,
but may not have been practised at this time.

Banking regulations None. No banks due to Islamic prohibition on
interest-bearing loans.

Economy

Taxation Taxes on land.

Coinage Indigenous coinage introduced in 1328.

Credit Credit and letters of exchange commonly used in business
transactions with northern Italian city-states.

Agricultural practices

Main crop Wheat

Irrigation Present

Fertilising Absent

Cropping system Unclear

Metallurgy
Base metals Bronze, iron and steel

Military equipment
Handheld weapons Maces, battle axes, daggers, straight swords, spears and polearms.

Armour Lamellar armour, helmets, chain mail, plate and scale armour, and wooden shields.

Projectiles Composite bows, crossbows, slings and javelins

Incendiaries Greek fire was known and projected through a *tufenk* blowpipe.

Long walls No long walls built.

Well-being
Life expectancy No data

Average adult stature No data

Irrigation & drinking water Pre-existing irrigation systems used; cities supplied with drinking water through fountains, cisterns and baths.

Health care Mixed. No centralised health-care system, but Sultan Bayezid I established a medical school and large hospital in 1400 CE.

Alimentary support Absent. Provided by religious institutions.

Famine relief Absent

(In)equalities
Social mobility *Madrasas* (Islamic schools) associated with mosques were open to boys and men of all classes and ethnicities, and graduates were considered worthy of joining the elites.

Occupational mobility Probably medium to high; no restrictions imposed on non-Muslims with regards to which professions they could practise.

Gender equality Unclear

Slavery State-owned enslaved soldiers fought in the military
(*janissaries*) and filled administrative roles; privately owned
enslaved people worked in agriculture and crafts.

Human sacrifice Absent. Forbidden by Islam.

Religion

Majority religious practice Sunni Islam

Early Modern: 1500 to 1800 CE

Ghana: Ashanti kingdom

In 1471 CE, Portuguese sailors reached the gold-producing region between the Comoé and Volta rivers in West Africa and established trade hubs, exchanging European goods for commodities such as gold and enslaved people. The Ashanti kingdom brought these hubs under their control. The king came from a royal clan and was elected by various officials, most notably the queen mother. He was a sacred person who could not be observed eating or drinking; he could not be spoken to or heard to speak. By the 19th century, the British had supplanted the Portuguese, and after failed attempts at reasserting independence, the entire region was declared a British territory in 1901.

General
Duration 1501–1901 CE
Language Ashanti (Akan)
Preceded by Denkyira
Succeeded by British Empire

Territory
Total area (km²) 240,000–260,000 in 1874 at the empire's height

People
Population 3m in 1874 at the empire's height
Largest city 10,000–20,000 (Kumasi)

Standing army 40,000–100,000

Social scale
Settlement hierarchy 1. Capital (Kumasi); 2. Towns; 3. Villages;
   4. Hamlets.
Administrative hierarchy 1. King (Asantehene); 2. Queen Mother
   (Asantehema), Council of Elders and other major officials;
   3. Provincial rulers; 4. Provincial councils; 5. Lineage chiefs;
   6. Village leaders.

Institutions
Legal code Absent. Customary law, informal legal system.
Bureaucracy Mixed. Appointed officials increasingly displaced
   hereditary officials.
Religious validation of rule Rulers were thought to have a special
   connection to the ancestors.
Property rights Mixed. Land formally owned by lineages rather than
   individuals, who only had usufruct rights.
Price controls Probably absent
Banking regulations Absent. No banking system.

Economy
Taxation Tax on gold dust; tolls; death duties imposed on the
   deceased's moveable property.
Coinage Absent
Credit Absent

Agricultural practices
Main crop Tubers (yams)
Irrigation Absent
Fertilising Present
Cropping system Swidden farming

Metallurgy
Base metals Bronze and iron

Military equipment
Handheld weapons Daggers and spears
Armour Shields and leather helmets
Projectiles Javelins, simple bows and firearms
Incendiaries Not known to have been used.
Long walls Not known to have been built.

Well-being
Life expectancy 30 years from birth in the early 20th century
Average adult stature 168 cm in the early 20th century
Irrigation & drinking water Absent
Health care Absent. No centralised state health-care service.
Alimentary support Probably absent. Probably no centralised
    alimentary support system.
Famine relief Probably absent. No centralised famine relief system.

(In)equalities
Social mobility Limited. Hereditary elite
Occupational mobility Limited. Present to some degree in cities.
Gender equality Gender complementarity rather than gender
    equality was the norm; most administrative roles closed to
    women.
Slavery Chattel slavery; war captives, rebels and criminals
    commonly enslaved.
Human sacrifice Mass sacrifices at elite funerals.

Religion
Majority religious practice Akan religion. Akans believed in a High
    God, Onyame, and a goddess of earth called Asase Yaa.

Iran: Safavid Empire

The Safavid was known as the "gunpowder empire" due to its use of artillery and muskets. On taking control of Persia, the Safavids declared Shi'a Islam the state religion, supplanting the Sunni Islam favoured by earlier rulers. Over time, the Safavid court asserted centralised control, developed a complex bureaucracy and acquired incredible wealth from a state monopoly over the silk trade. This trade led to diplomatic relations with European powers. Imperial decline in the 17th century, combined with the ascendancy of European and Ottoman power, culminated in the 1724 Treaty of Constantinople, which divided Safavid territory between the Ottoman and Russian empires.

General
Duration 1501–1722 CE
Language Persian (Indo-European)
Preceded by Ak Koyunlu tribal confederation
Succeeded by Afsharid dynasty

Territory
Total area (km²) 2.7m

People
Population 9m
Largest city 200,000 (Isfahan)
Standing army 90,000–120,000

Social scale

Settlement hierarchy 1. Capital; 2. Large cities; 3. Small cities;
   4. Towns; 5. Villages; 6. Hamlets.

Administrative hierarchy 1. Shah; 2. Grand Vizier; 3. State council;
   4. Central administration; 5. Provincial governors; 6. Local
   government.

Institutions

Legal code Secular law and religious law

Bureaucracy Administrative roles were salaried but hereditary.

Religious validation of rule Safavid rulership partly rested on pre-
   Islamic notions of divine kingship.

Property rights Absent. The shah claimed ownership of all land.

Price controls Integral part of famine relief measures.

Banking regulations None

Economy

Taxation Taxes on land; trade thoroughly taxed through its
   movement, with customs fees and road tolls and a special duty
   (*tamgha*) that was placed on commodities at the border.

Coinage Silver *tangers*, *tumans* and *dinars*; copper coins minted and
   used within regions; a number of Shahs also minted a gold coin
   called the *ashrafi*.

Credit Reputable merchants carried out loan extensions, the
   discounting and collection of bills of exchange, the acceptance
   of deposits, and transfer of funds.

Agricultural practices

Main crop Wheat

Irrigation Present

Fertilising Present

Cropping system Fallowing, two-field rotation and nitrogen-fixing
   crops.

Metallurgy
Metals Bronze, iron and steel

Military equipment
Handheld weapons Maces, battle axes, scimitars and lances
Armour Light armour made from leather, wool, silk and felt; wooden
    shields, helmets, breastplates, limb protection and chain mail.
Projectiles Thrown spears, composite bows, crossbows and muskets
Incendiaries Siege artillery. Glass bottles filled with flaming oil.
Long walls Not known to have been built.

Well-being
Life expectancy No data
Average adult stature No data
Irrigation & drinking water Government-managed *qanat* system since
    Sassanid times.
Health care One or two hospitals in each large city.
Alimentary support Unclear
Famine relief Price control measures in times of crisis; state
    granaries established at villages throughout the realm to
    guarantee regular supply to the capital.

(In)equalities
Social mobility Official positions were awarded on the basis of merit,
    not birth, regardless of class or ethnicity; the original Safavid
    aristocracy experienced a progressive loss of power and
    influence.
Occupational mobility Probably present
Gender equality Elite women inherited land, made charitable
    endowments, owned caravanserais and wielded great political
    influence; even commoner women took part in pilgrimages,
    rallies and riots, and it was not uncommon for them to be
    merchants.

Slavery Shah Tahmasp (r. 1524–76) is known to have enslaved the
border peoples, whose descendants were also enslaved.

Human sacrifice Absent. Forbidden by Islam.

Religion

Majority religious practice Shia Islam

India: Mughal Empire

Founded by Babur, who invaded India from Central Asia and deployed artillery to defeat the Delhi sultanate, the Mughal Empire was one of the largest states in premodern history, covering most of the Indian subcontinent. The Mughals established an efficient taxation system administered by local tax farmers, and relied on salaried civil and military officials rather than titled nobility. Under their rule, India became a centre of global trade, its manufactured goods, especially cotton textiles, in demand from China to western Europe. The importance of Indian commerce in Europe led to the formation of the British East India Company, which wrested control of the subcontinent from the Mughals in the mid-19th century.

General
Duration 1526–1858
Languages Persian (Indo-European); Urdu (Indo-European)
Preceded by Delhi sultanate; Sind Empire; Vijayanagara Empire
(India); Timurid Empire (Central Asia).
Succeeded by British Empire (India); Durrani Empire (Central Asia)

Territory
Total area (km²) 3.2–4.5m

People
Population 110–150m
Largest city 400,000 (Delhi in 1650 during a visit from the royal
court, which moved regularly from city to city).
Standing army 102,000

Social scale

Settlement hierarchy 1. Capital; 2. Provincial centres; 3. Towns; 4. Villages.

Administrative hierarchy 1. Emperor; 2. Chief minister (*wakil*); 3. Subahdar officials; 4. Sarkar officials; 5. Paragana officials; 6. Village officials; 7. Village record keeper.

Institutions

Legal code Twelve Ordinances of Jahangir, established in 1605.

Bureaucracy Professional

Religious validation of rule Cult of the emperor as *linsan-e-Kamil* (the Universal Man), *Murshid* (spiritual director) and "Shadow of God"; rulers also sought to emphasise link to Timur (1336–1406 CE), founder of the Timurid Empire.

Property rights Mixed. All land owned by the state, but the performance of administrative and military duties could be exchanged for land usufruct.

Price controls No data

Banking regulations No data

Economy

Taxation Tax on land; Emperor Akbar abolished the *jizya* tax that Islamic rulers usually imposed on non-Muslims.

Coinage Silver *rupya*; 0.30 *rupyas* = 25.11 kg wheat (increased to 6.66 *rupyas* during famines). Monthly wage in *rupyas* of an unskilled labourer in Agra was 1.5 in 1595 CE; 3.2 in 1637.

Credit Present

Agricultural practices

Main crops Wheat, rice and pulses

Irrigation Present

Fertilising Probably present

Cropping system Nitrogen-fixing crops

Metallurgy
Base metals Bronze, iron and steel

Military equipment
Handheld weapons War clubs, battle axes, daggers, swords, short
   spears, halberds and two-handed swords.
Armour Shields, helmets, chain mail, plate armour and limb
   protection.
Projectiles Javelins, slings, *chakrams* (steel discs), composite bows,
   crossbows and muskets.
Incendiaries Gunpowder bombs, incendiary canisters and rockets
   bombs, siege artillery.
Long walls Not known to have been built.

Well-being
Life expectancy 25–35 years from birth
Average adult stature 158 cm (male)
Irrigation & drinking water Canals, cisterns, channels, dams, ponds,
   wells, etc. built to capture and transport river and monsoon
   rains.
Health care Hospitals built by state and private parties; Jahangir (r.
   1605–27) proclaimed that hospitals should be built in every city
   of the empire.
Alimentary support Provided by hospitals.
Famine relief Emperor Akbar set up a system of district granaries to
   respond to famine; ad hoc distribution of money and food in
   times of famine.

(In)equalities
Social mobility Hereditary elite. Caste system for Hindu majority.
Occupational mobility Absent. Caste system for Hindu majority.
Gender equality Present to different extents; the major ideological
   systems all fostered gender inequality.

Slavery In 1562 CE Akbar officially ended the enslavement of war
   captives; enslaved people still commonly kept by aristocracy.
Human sacrifice Absent. Forbidden by Islam.

Religion
Majority religious practices Sunni Islam; Hinduism; Jainism

Ecuador: Shuar peoples, Spanish colonial period

The Shuar peoples (also known as the Jivaro), have for centuries inhabited the forested foothills of the Andes near the modern-day border between Ecuador and Peru. Authority among different Shuar groups has traditionally resided in "big men" – renowned warriors or shamans who had earned reputations for friendliness, honesty and generosity. Shuar religion centred on an impersonal sacred force called *tsarutama* – similar to the *mana* of many Polynesian faiths – which could be good or evil, and which accumulated to individuals through deeds such as bravery in warfare and generosity to neighbours. The Shuar resisted Incan and then European domination, until their incorporation into Ecuador in 1930.

General
Duration 1530–1840
Languages Jivaro or Shuar (Jivaroan)
Preceded by Pre-colonial Jivaro peoples
Succeeded by Jivaro, post-colonial Ecuadorian period

Territory
Total area (km²) 16 (estimate based on the fact that villages were typically 4 km apart).

People
Population 300 (population of a village)
Largest city 300. No true cities, probably no villages with more than 300 inhabitants.

Standing army 500. No standing armies; number provided is an estimate for the size of raiding parties.

Social scale
Settlement hierarchy Villages only
Administrative hierarchy 1. Headmen doubling as occasional ad hoc supra-local leaders; 2. Chiefs (*kurakas*).

Institutions
Legal code Absent
Bureaucracy Absent
Religious validation of rule Shamans were often considered chiefs (*kurakas*) due to their spiritual power.
Property rights Absent
Price controls Absent
Banking regulations None

Economy
Taxation Present. Imposed by colonial authorities.
Coinage Absent
Credit Present

Agricultural practices
Main crop Cassava
Irrigation Absent
Fertilising Present
Cropping system Swidden farming

Metallurgy
Base metals Absent. Copper weaponry acquired through trade.

Military equipment
Handheld weapons Battle axes, machetes and thrusting spears
Armour Leather and wooden shields

Projectiles Blow guns, poisoned darts; *atlatls* up until the late 17th
century; javelins.

Incendiaries Not known to have been used.

Long walls Not known to have been built.

Well-being

Life expectancy No data

Average adult stature 167 cm (male)

Irrigation & drinking water Absent

Health care Absent. No state existed to provide centralised health-
care service.

Alimentary support Absent. No state existed to provide centralised
alimentary support service.

Famine relief Absent. No state existed to provide centralised famine
relief service.

(In)equalities

Social mobility None. No true social classes.

Occupational mobility None. The Jivaros were almost invariably
subsistence horticulturalists.

Gender equality Division of labour based on gender; polygyny
common; leadership positions reserved for men.

Slavery Absent. War captives were not usually enslaved as their
decapitated heads were made into trophies.

Human sacrifice War captives often ritually killed.

Religion

Majority religious practices Jivaro religion; Shamanism

France: Bourbon kingdom

The House of Bourbon ruled France from the death of the Valois King Henry III in 1589, who left no heir, to the French Revolution. The Bourbons came to power amid the Wars of Religion between Catholics and Protestants. Bureaucracy, centralised taxation and colonial conquests in the Americas fuelled its rise as an imperial power in the 17th century. The peak of the French kingdom was achieved under the "Sun King", Louis XIV (r. 1643–1715). The palace of Versailles, then the largest building in Europe, was constructed under the Sun King's guidance in the 1670s and 1680s. He also nullified the Edict of Nantes, turning France once more into a Catholic kingdom.

General
Duration 1589–1789
Language French (Indo-European)
Preceded by Valois kingdom (France)
Succeeded by Revolutionary period (France)

Territory
Total area (km²) 930,000 in 1600; 2.6m in 1650; 2–2.5m in 1700

People
Population 18.5m in 1600; 21m in 1650; 25.3m in 1700; 28.5m in 1789
Largest city 245,000 in 1600; 455,000 in 1650; 600,000 in 1700
   (Paris).
Standing army 50,000 in 1600; 400,000–500,000 in 1700

Social scale

Settlement hierarchy 1. Capital (Paris); 2. Provincial capitals and
colonial centres; 3. Cities; 4. Towns; 5. Villages; 6. Hamlets.

Administrative hierarchy 1. King; 2. High council (*conseil d'en haut*);
3. Provincial superintendent; 4. *Généralité* superintendent;
5. Sub-delegate, city and provincial governors; 6. *Prévôt*.

Institutions

Legal code Known as the Code Michaud.

Bureaucracy Professional

Religious validation of rule King supported by church; Louis XIV (the
"Sun King") placed monarchy at the centre of state ideology.

Property rights Present

Price controls Price of salt fixed.

Banking regulations Unclear

Economy

Taxation Rigorous tax system which the nobility could evade
through tax exemption privileges.

Coinage Silver *livre tournois*, worth 20 *sous* or 240 *deniers*; two failed
attempts to introduce paper currency.

Credit Present

Agricultural practices

Main crop Wheat

Irrigation Absent

Fertilising Present

Cropping system Three-field rotation and nitrogen-fixing crops

Metallurgy

Base metals Bronze, iron and steel

Military equipment

Handheld weapons Swords, sabres, halberds, spontoons and
bayonets.

Armour Breastplates, cuirasses or leather waistcoats, steel or brass
helmets, limb protection.

Projectiles Carbines, muskets and pistols

Incendiaries Grenades and siege artillery

Long walls Not known to have been built.

Well-being

Life expectancy 25–28 years from birth

Average adult stature 172 cm (male); 158 cm (female)

Irrigation & drinking water Particularly extensive irrigation works in
the south of France; wells and public drinking fountains
common in cities.

Health care Absent. State did not provide health-care services, but
hospitals run by privates or church were common in cities.

Alimentary support Absent. According to the Edict of Moulins (1566),
local communities (particularly local church authorities) were
responsible for the relief of the poor.

Famine relief Absent

(In)equalities

Social mobility Mixed. It was possible for commoners to enter the
ranks of the hereditary nobility.

Occupational mobility Present

Gender equality 25% of women were literate. Women could own and
manage property; Louis XIV attempted to restrict female control
over property and marriage choices and created a prison at the
Salpêtrière specifically for women.

Slavery Present in large numbers in colonial territories. Slave trade
briefly abolished in 1794 before reinstatement.

Human sacrifice Absent. Forbidden by Christianity.

Religion

Majority religious practice Roman Catholicism

Japan: Tokugawa Shogunate

The Tokugawa Shogunate, also known as the Edo period, began
with Tokugawa Ieyasu's victory at the Battle of Sekigahara and his
appointment as "shogun". Although the emperor remained the
nominal head of state, the shoguns ruled Japan in every other
sense. The Tokogawa pursued a policy of "orthodoxy and stability"
aimed at consolidating their own power and suppressing potential
rivals, which enabled the family to rule for nearly three centuries.
A side-effect of this long and prosperous peace was that military
expertise decayed, with many of the samurai becoming bureaucra-
tised – a development that contributed to the romanticisation of the
old warrior ideal. Eventually, economic difficulties and the threat
of Western encroachment helped to bring about the end of the
Tokugawa Shogunate. The period closed with the resignation of the
last Tokugawa shogun in 1867 and the imperial restoration in 1868.

General
Duration 1603–1868
Language Japanese (Japonic)
Preceded by Azuchi–Momoyama period
Succeeded by Meiji period

Territory
Total area (km²) 295,000

People
Population 25m in 1650; 28m in 1750; 32m in 1850
Largest city 570,000 in 1678; 1.3m in 1720; 1.4m in 1800 (Tokyo [Edo])

Standing army 125,000; size of Tokugawa forces mobilised to defeat the Shimabara Rebellion.

Social scale

Settlement hierarchy 1. Capital (Edo); 2. Large cities; 3. Castle towns and market towns; 4. Port towns; 5. Temple/shrine towns; 6. Villages.

Administrative hierarchy 1. Shogun; 2. Senior councillors (*roju*); 3. Junior councillors (*wakadoshiyori*); 4. Lesser central administrators; 5. Hereditary lords (*daimyo*); 6. Provincial officials; 7. Lesser provincial administrators.

Institutions

Legal code Present

Bureaucracy Professional

Religious validation of rule Shogun wished to be known as a benevolent ruler (*jinkun*), based on Buddhist ideals of compassion (*jihi*) and neo-Confucian precepts of benevolent government (*jinsi*).

Property rights Present

Price controls Present

Banking regulations Unclear

Economy

Taxation Main source of state revenue came from a land tax from lands directly administered by the state.

Coinage Gold, silver and bronze coins that behaved as separate currencies.

Credit Thousands of banks called *ryogae* existed, mostly based in Osaka and Edo.

Agricultural practices

Main crop Rice

Irrigation Present
Fertilising Present
Cropping system Crop rotation

Metallurgy
Base metals Bronze, iron and steel

Military equipment
Handheld weapons Iron clubs (*kanabou*), battle axes, daggers, curved
swords, spears (*yari*), polearms (*naginata*), truncheons (*jittejutsu*)
and staffs (*bojutsu*).
Armour Helmets, shields, breastplates, limb protection and chain
mail, laminar and scale armour.
Projectiles Composite bows; gunpowder weapons known in this
period.
Incendiaries *Hiyaho* were guns that shot flaming arrows; *rokudama*
were early hand grenades.
Long walls Not known to have been built.

Well-being
Life expectancy 27 years from birth (male); 25 years (female)
Average adult stature 157 cm (male); 148 cm (female)
Irrigation & drinking water Irrigation systems, such as canals with
locks and sluice gates, were built and maintained; cities were
provided with drinking water.
Health care Unclear. State founded a hospital in Tokyo, but unclear
to what extent this was part of wider effort to provide health-
care service.
Alimentary support Shogun was expected to provide "lord's relief"
(*osukui*) to the needy, particularly after natural disasters.
Famine relief Shogun was expected to provide "lord's relief" (*osukui*)
to the needy, particularly after natural disasters.

(In)equalities

Social mobility Hereditary elite

Occupational mobility Limited

Gender equality Lower-class women experienced greater equality
and had a greater role in community life than women of the
ruling classes, where polygamy was practised and women were
discouraged from participating in public life.

Slavery Slave trade abolished in 1590.

Human sacrifice Absent

Religion

Majority religious practices Shinto; Mahayana Buddhism; Neo-
Confucianism

USA: Iliniouek confederation

The Iliniouek (also known as Inoca, Illiniwek and Illini) occupied the territory to the east of the Mississippi river, bounded by Lake Michigan, the Ohio river and the Wabash. Illini-speaking groups probably arrived in this area just before the 16th century, possibly migrating from the Lake Erie basin and displacing previous inhabitants such as the Oneota. Despite the use of the term "confederacy", there is no indication in the historical record of formal inter-tribal political organisations like those of the Haudenosaunee confederation. Political leadership in each community was provided by "peace chiefs" who played important diplomatic roles but had little formal authority, and war chiefs, who organised raids on other settlements. Despite territorial and political incursions by French and later British forces, Ilinouek rule only formally ended with their displacement at the hands of an expanding United States of America.

General
Duration 1640–1778
Language Miami Illinois (Algonquin)
Preceded by Oneota cultural complex
Succeeded by USA

Territory
Total area (km²) 14,000–19,000. No single unitary state; this is the size of a typical Illinois society.

People
Population 8,000–12,000 in 1700; 300–600 in 1778

Largest city 2,000–3,000. No true cities; estimate for a typical larger
  settlement.
Standing army No data

Social scale
Settlement hierarchy Semi-permanent villages only
Administrative hierarchy 1. Peace chief; 2. Village chief.

Institutions
Legal code Absent
Bureaucracy Absent
Religious validation of rule Chiefs were chosen based on their ability
  to maintain social well-being; war chiefs were thought to have
  particularly powerful spirit animals (*manitou*).
Property rights Probably absent
Price controls Absent
Banking regulations Absent

Economy
Taxation Absent
Coinage Absent
Credit Probably absent

Agricultural practices
Main crop Maize
Irrigation Absent
Fertilising Absent
Cropping system Two-field rotation and nitrogen-fixing crops

Metallurgy
Metals Absent

Military equipment

Handheld weapons Wood or antler sword-like clubs for bludgeoning; knives and hatchets.

Armour Bison-hide shields

Projectiles Simple bows and muskets

Incendiaries Not known to have been used.

Long walls Not known to have been built.

Well-being

Life expectancy No data

Average adult stature No data

Irrigation & drinking water Absent. Not state provided.

Health care Absent

Alimentary support Absent

Famine relief Absent

(In)equalities

Social mobility Egalitarian

Occupational mobility Egalitarian

Gender equality Men had considerable power over women in terms of arranging their marriage, though women could become shamans and chiefs.

Slavery Chattel slavery; female and child war captives enslaved.

Human sacrifice Absent

Religion

Majority religious practice Illinois religion. Supreme god known as the Master of Life; warfare rituals known, as well as shamanic practices and celebratory dances.

China: Qing dynasty

The final dynasty of China's 2,000-year imperial period, the Qing were Manchu descendants of the rulers of the state of Jin in what is today northeast China and northern Korea. Supplanting the Ming dynasty in 1644, the Qing reached their height in the late 18th century. However, British traders illegally trafficking opium triggered the Opium Wars in the 1830s, and the empire was also wracked by the 14-year Taiping Rebellion, which caused 30 million deaths. By the late 19th century, European powers seized coastal territory, contributing to the 1900 Boxer Rebellion. The Qing were finally overthrown in the Revolution of 1911, which established the Republic of China.

General
Duration 1644–1912
Languages Chinese (Sino-Tibetan); Manchu (Tungusic)
Preceded by Ming dynasty
Succeeded by Republic of China

Territory
Total area (km²) 13.1m in 1644–1796; 11.3m in 1796–1912

People
Population 100–140m in 1700; 295m in 1800; 334–48m in 1900
Largest city 670,000–820,000 in 1700; 1m in 1800; 1.1m in 1900 (Beijing).
Standing army 820,000–900,000. Eight Banner Army (220,000 troops in total) garrisoned in Beijing, Manchuria and in most

important cities; Green Standard Army (over 600,000 troops) responsible for law and order at local level.

Social scale

Settlement hierarchy 1. Capital (Beijing); 2. Provincial centre; 3. Prefectural centre; 4. County centre; 5. Town; 6. Village.

Administrative hierarchy 1. Emperor; 2. Central administration; 3. Provincial governors; 4. Prefects; 5. County governors; 6. District magistrate.

Institutions

Legal code Present

Bureaucracy Professional. Bureaucrats recruited through demanding examination process.

Religious validation of rule Ideological legitimation through the Mandate of Heaven.

Property rights Present

Price controls Probably present

Banking regulations Probably present

Economy

Taxation Taxes on property, land and sales; poll tax.

Coinage Silver *taels*, made by independent silversmiths, with value determined by weight; state-issued paper money during the reigns of Xunzhi (1644–61) and Xianfeng (1851–61). In the mid-18th century, 1 kg of rice in Canton or millet in Beijing cost about 0.024 *taels*. In 1813, the average daily wage of an unskilled labourer in most provinces was 0.04 *taels*.

Credit Present

Agricultural practices

Main crops Wheat and rice. Wheat was the main crop in the north, rice in the south.

Irrigation Present
Fertilising Present
Cropping system Crop rotation

Metallurgy
Base metals Bronze, iron and steel

Military equipment
Handheld weapons Swords, daggers, spears and polearms
Armour Protective jackets made from bark-pulp paper; brigandines
(metal plates attached to fabric); rattan-cane shields; helmets,
limb protection, breastplates.
Projectiles Matchlocks, arquebuses, crossbows, composite bows and
grappling hooks.
Incendiaries Rockets
Long walls Great Wall of China

Well-being
Life expectancy 35 years from birth
Average adult stature 167 cm (male); 153 cm (female)
Irrigation & drinking water New irrigation works; water delivered to
cities from reservoirs, lakes or rivers using structures such as
canals, aqueducts and culverts.
Health care Absent. Not provided by the state, but by private
shantang and *shanhui* ("benevolent society") institutions.
Alimentary support Absent. Not provided by the state, but by private
charities and Buddhist monasteries.
Famine relief Absent. Not provided by the state, but by regional
authorities working with charities, as well as Buddhist
monasteries.

(In)equalities

Social mobility Examination system opened administrative roles to men of all backgrounds but the very lowest.

Occupational mobility Examination system opened administrative roles to men of all backgrounds but the very lowest.

Gender equality Legal rights differed on the basis of gender; administrative roles reserved for men.

Slavery In the early 17th century the Yongzheng emperor carried out a programme to emancipate most agricultural serfs and enslaved people.

Human sacrifice Absent

Religion

Majority religious practices Confucianism; Buddhism; Daoism; Chinese folk religion.

Borneo: Dayak peoples, pre-Brooke Raj period

The Dayak people, also known as the Iban, have lived in western Kalimantan, Borneo, for centuries, usually in autonomous 500-person strong longhouse communities. The Dayak eschew permanent leaders: groups of family authorities direct the affairs of each house, and specialists such as warriors, storytellers and seers are able to earn influence. The Iban aggressively expanded their territory through the 17th, 18th and 19th centuries, practising headhunting and engaging in the slave trade. Their expansion was checked in 1841 by the British adventurer James Brooke, of the Brooke Raj, who colonised parts of Borneo under the British flag. The British maintained control until Brunei's independence in 1984.

General
Duration 1650–1841
Language Iban (Austronesian)
Preceded by Early Iban settlement
Succeeded by Brooke Raj British colonial period

Territory
Total area (km²) No data

People
Population <500. Estimate for average tribal size.
Largest city <500. No true cities; in the 20th century, larger Iban longhouse communities had about 500 inhabitants.
Standing army No standing armies, only ad hoc raiding parties, and there are no estimates for the latter.

Social scale

Settlement hierarchy Longhouse communities only

Administrative hierarchy Village headmen (*tuai rumah*) only

Institutions

Legal code Absent

Bureaucracy Absent

Religious or other validation of rule Informal leaders owed their authority to age and personal qualities.

Property rights Absent. Wealth was transmitted within longhouse lineages.

Price controls Absent

Banking regulations None. No banks.

Economy

Taxation Absent

Coinage Absent

Credit Absent

Agricultural practices

Main crop Rice

Irrigation Absent

Fertilising Present

Cropping system Swidden farming

Metallurgy

Base metal Iron

Military equipment

Handheld weapons Thrusting spears and swords

Armour Wooden shields; cloth, bear- or leopard-skin *baju* (war jackets); wicker skull caps.

Projectiles 8-foot-long blowpipe that could fire darts accurately over

20 metres; *slighi* (javelin) with a fire-hardened point thrown on approach to enemy.

Incendiaries Not known to have been used.

Long walls Not known to have been built.

Well-being

Life expectancy 44 years average age at death

Average adult stature 159 cm

Irrigation & drinking water Absent

Health care Absent. No state existed to provide centralised health-care system.

Alimentary support Absent. No state existed to provide centralised alimentary support system.

Famine relief Absent. No state existed to provide centralised famine relief system.

(In)equalities

Social mobility Absent. No true social classes.

Occupational mobility Absent. Most Iban were subsistence farmers.

Gender equality Leadership positions closed to women, though women had important roles in ritual and economic activity and were typically consulted in group decision-making.

Slavery Chattel slavery; war captives and debtors were usually enslaved.

Human sacrifice War captives occasionally sacrificed.

Religion

Majority religious practices Iban religion; Shamanism

Papua New Guinea: Orokaiva peoples

The "Orokaiva" is an umbrella term used to describe numerous culturally similar groups, including the Aiga, Binandele, Hunjara, Mambare and Wasida, who inhabit the Northern Province of Papua New Guinea. Primarily comprising subsistence farmers but also hunters and fishermen, Orokaiva society was organised around relatively autonomous clans led by "big men" (*embo dambo*) and elders who gained respect and influence based on their personal qualities. Clan affiliation was inherited through the paternal line and each clan claimed common descent from a semi-mythical heroic ancestor. The Orokaiva formally became part of the British Empire when the island was annexed in 1888, until independence in 1975.

General
Duration 1734–1884
Language Orokaiva (Papuan)
Preceded by Early Orokiava settlement
Succeeded by British colonial Papua New Guinea

Territory
Total area (km²) 1,000. No single unitary state; estimate for average tribe territory.

People
Population 750. No single unitary state; estimate for average tribe population.
Largest city 600–800. No true cities; estimate for larger villages.
Standing army Absent

Social scale
Settlement hierarchy Villages only

Administrative hierarchy 1. Leaders of ad hoc alliances; 2. Big men (*embo dambo*) and village elders.

Institutions
Legal code Absent. The *igege* were a collection of moral taboos against stealing, adultery, violence and the infringement of certain property rights.

Bureaucracy Absent

Religious or other validation of rule *Embo dambo* depended on the support of his wives and the young men attached to his household; sponsored pig feasts to demonstrate generosity.

Property rights Unclear. Individual garden plots appear to have been considered private property, though this is not entirely clear.

Price controls Absent

Banking regulations Absent. No banking system.

Economy
Taxation Absent

Coinage Absent

Credit Absent. No banking system or similar.

Agricultural practices
Main crop Taro

Irrigation Absent

Fertilising Present

Cropping system Swidden farming

Metallurgy
Base metals Absent

Military equipment
Handheld weapons Spears, war clubs and battle axes
Armour Wooden shields
Projectiles Thrown spears
Incendiaries Not known to have been used.
Long walls Not known to have been built.

Well-being
Life expectancy 40–45 years average age at death
Average adult stature 160 cm
Irrigation & drinking water Absent
Health care Absent
Alimentary support Absent
Famine relief Absent

(In)equalities
Social mobility Egalitarian
Occupational mobility Egalitarian
Gender equality Gendered division of labour; women could not become tribe leaders (*embo dambo*).
Slavery Women and children frequently taken as war captives.
Human sacrifice Unclear. Evidence that occasionally murder was avenged by killing and eating the culprit, perhaps a form of sacrifice.

Religion
Majority religious practices Orokaiva religion; animistic beliefs

Micronesia: Truk peoples

The Truk peoples settled on the Chuuk Islands (Chuuk meaning "high mountains"), part of modern Micronesia, in the 1st century CE. The islands were more fragmented than contemporary Micronesian societies. Each Truk clan was led by the oldest (or most senior) man according to matrilineal descent. In addition to inherited status, his authority derived from his knowledge of the intentions of spirits and ability to wield *manaman*, a divine energy. Households were led by an elder woman and two younger women of childbearing age together with their husbands. Each lineage retained the right to work and reside on its land, but in return was responsible for preparing food for the chief. The islands' first contact with Europeans came in 1528 CE, when they were sighted by Spanish explorers.

General
Duration 1775–1886
Language Chuukese (Austronesian)
Preceded by Moen culture
Succeeded by Spanish colonial Chuuk Islands

Territory
Total area (km²) No data. Islands cover 127 km² in total; size of a typical region under the control of a clan chief is not known.

People
Population 500–1000. Estimate of size of average tribal group.
Largest city 100–200. No true cities; estimate for a typical larger settlement.

Standing army No data

Social scale
Settlement hierarchy Hamlets only
Administrative hierarchy 1. Clan chief; 2. Head of household.

Institutions
Legal code Absent
Bureaucracy Absent
Religious validation of rule A chief's authority depended on association with spirits of the sky, sea and land, and his command of the sorcery they permitted.
Property rights Land held both by individuals and corporate descent groups.
Price controls Absent
Banking regulations Absent

Economy
Taxation Absent
Coinage Absent
Credit Absent

Agricultural practices
Main crop Breadfruit
Irrigation Absent
Fertilising Present
Cropping system Swidden farming

Metallurgy
Base metals Absent

Military equipment
Handheld weapons Clubs and spears
Armour Not known to have been used.

Projectiles Slings

Incendiaries Not known to have been used.

Long walls Not known to have been built.

Well-being

Life expectancy 40–45 years average age at death

Average adult stature 167 cm (male); 164 cm (female) (estimates from mid-20th century).

Irrigation & drinking water Absent

Health care Absent

Alimentary support Unclear

Famine relief Unclear. Surplus from breadfruit harvest stored in communal pits for later use; use of this food resource was controlled by the chief.

(In)equalities

Social mobility Hereditary elite

Occupational mobility Limited

Gender equality Division of labour based on gender; women could own property without husband's consent; leaders mostly male.

Slavery Absent

Human sacrifice War captives were offered to the god Paladiu.

Religion

Majority religious practice Chuukese religion. Spirits were used for magical spells, medicines and rituals intended to influence all aspects of life from house building and courtship to politics and war.

India: A'chik peoples

Commonly known as the Garos, the *A'chik Manderang* ("hill people")
are the long-time inhabitants of the Garo Hills in the Meghalaya
district of northeast India. Though it is unknown precisely when
the *A'chik* settled in their present location, it is believed that they
migrated there from Tibet. They had little contact with their
neighbours before 1775, when local *zamindars* (Indian land-owning
nobility) led expeditions into the hills. Organised into matrilineal
clans, *A'chik* chiefs had little power beyond religious functions and
resolving minor disputes under the guidance of village elders. The
British occupied the district in 1867 and succeeded in extracting
resources from the *A'chik* by promoting cash-crop agriculture.

General
Duration 1775–1867
Language Garo (Sino-Tibetan)
Preceded by Early Garo settlement
Succeeded by British Empire

Territory
Total area (km²) No data

People
Population 2,000–3,000. No single unitary society; estimate for a
    typical larger settlement/village cluster.
Largest city 2,000–3,000. No true cities; estimate for a typical larger
    settlement/village cluster.
Standing army Absent

Social scale
Settlement hierarchy 1. Villages; 2. Hamlets.
Administrative hierarchy 1. Village head (*nokma*); 2. Village elders.

Institutions
Legal code Absent
Bureaucracy Absent
Religious or other validation of rule *Nokma* often not greatly
distinguishable in status from others, and often followed
instructions of village. elders.
Property rights Mixed. Land was owned by matrilineal clans and
allotted to individual households.
Price controls Absent
Banking regulations Absent. No banking system.

Economy
Taxation Absent
Coinage Absent
Credit Absent. No banking system or similar.

Agricultural practices
Main crops Rice, tubers
Irrigation Absent
Fertilising Present
Cropping system Swidden farming

Metallurgy
Base metal Iron

Military equipment
Handheld weapons Axes (*mongreng, banuk, dao*); thrusting spears
with a five-foot bamboo shaft and an imported iron head;
swords.

Armour Three-foot concave shield made of wood or hide stretched over a wooden frame.

Projectiles Simple bows

Incendiaries Not known to have been used.

Long walls Not known to have been built.

Well-being

Life expectancy No data

Average adult stature 156 cm (male); 147 cm (female)

Irrigation & drinking water Absent

Health care Absent

Alimentary support Absent

Famine relief Absent

(In)equalities

Social mobility Egalitarian

Occupational mobility Egalitarian

Gender equality Gendered division of labour; *nokmas* only known to have been men.

Slavery Enslaved people taken in warfare were used for domestic and agricultural labour.

Human sacrifice Enslaved people sacrificed at funerals.

Religion

Majority religious practice Garo religion. *Kamals* (village priests) solved problems caused by evil spirits, healed people, watched the dead and acted as midwives.

USA: Kingdom of Hawaii

A war chief and keeper of the war god Kūka'ilimoku, Kamehameha rebelled against King Kīwala'ō in 1782 and seized the Kohala and Kona districts of the archipelago's Big Island. Over the next three decades, Kamehameha waged military campaigns to unify the archipelago (minus Kaua'i and Ni'ihau). *Mana*, the life-giving power emanating from gods and ancestors, was central to Hawaiian religion and manifested in displays of power, strength and skill. But it did not flow equally to all. Over time, chiefs sought to monopolise *mana* and the authority and prestige that came with it, leading to an increasingly hierarchical society.

General
Duration 1778–1898
Language Hawaiian (Austronesian)
Preceded by Pre-contact Hawaii
Succeeded by USA

Territory
Total area (km²) 11,000 in 1778; 15,000 in 1795; 16,600 in 1810

People
Population 60,000–150,000 in 1778; 140,000–180,000 in 1810
Largest city No data
Standing army 36,000–48,000 (largest fielded army)

Social scale
Settlement hierarchy 1. Royal/chiefly palace; 2. Dispersed
    households.

Administrative hierarchy 1. King (*ali'i nui*); 2. Royal advisor
(*kālaimoku*); 3. Governor; district chief (*ali'i-ai-moku*); 4. Lower
chiefs (*ali'i-'ai-ahupua'a*); 5. Land managers (*konohiki*).

Institutions

Legal code Absent. There was a body of customary law governing
rights to water, fishing and land. But there were no written,
formal law codes.

Bureaucracy Stewards (*konohiki*) formed a sort of "incipient
bureaucracy" of specialists in memorising genealogies,
traditions and other information. Seem not to have been full
time or professionalised.

Religious validation of rule Hawaiian kings ruled as divine figures, in
control of the most *mana* (the manifestation of cosmic power).

Property rights Limited. All land in theory belonged to the *ali'i
nui* (king), who distributed it to chiefs and allies. Land grants
awarded allowed occupants limited right of usufruct, partibility
and exclusivity, but with restrictions on use.

Price controls Probably absent. No solid evidence for market
exchange.

Banking regulations Absent. Nothing akin to banks or
institutionalised monetary activity.

Economy

Taxation Tribute. Occupiers of land owed *corvée* labour and in-kind
tax (tribute) to chiefs and the king, which was as much as
two-thirds of production.

Coinage Absent. Wage labour not practised. Limited redistribution of
food and goods collected as tribute to chiefs and commoners.

Credit Probably absent. No evidence for credit instruments or debt
structures.

Agricultural practices
Main crops Sweet potato and taro
Irrigation Present
Fertilising Present
Cropping system Dry-field and irrigated farming

Metallurgy
Metals Indigenous metallurgy absent but metal items brought to the islands by European traders.

Military equipment
Handheld weapons Spears, war clubs
Armour No evidence for armour
Projectiles Javelins, slings; firearms purchased from Europeans
Incendiaries Siege cannon
Long walls Not known to have been built.

Well-being
Life expectancy No data
Average adult stature No data
Irrigation & drinking water Irrigation infrastructure was extensive, including water-diversion walls for dryland agriculture and pondfields for taro. Drinking water not provided.
Health care Absent. Not provided. Professional priests with medicinal roles (*kahuna lapa'au*).
Alimentary support Mixed. Chiefs provided storage of provisions for redistribution, but mostly as gifts to other chiefs and retainers and not based on need; little given to commoners.
Famine relief Chiefs expected to distribute stored provisions in times of great need, but little evidence for large-scale relief efforts in practice.

(In)equalities

Social mobility Hereditary elites

Occupational mobility Hereditary adoption of crafts and professions

Gender equality Elite women could serve as priests and hold land; women faced restrictions on diet and there were other taboos. Men and women did not eat together.

Slavery Largely absent. The majority of people, *Maka'āinana* (commoners), were free, but there was also a subordinate class of people, *Kauwā*, who were often used as human sacrifice.

Human sacrifice Victims were selected from war captives and *Kauwā*, more rarely elites and commoners. Practice ended in 1804 under the influence of Christianity.

Religion

Majority religious practice Traditional Polynesian religion. Traditional polytheistic ritual system based on idea of *mana*; Kapu system stressed normative behaviours and responsibility of chiefs to protect *mana*.

Thailand: Rattanakosin kingdom

Rama I Chakri emerged as the leader of the Ayutthayan nobility following the Burmese destruction of Ayutthaya in modern-day Thailand in 1767. He moved the capital to Bangkok, then known as Rattanakosin or Krungthep, and founded his kingdom. The Rattanakosin were ruled by a Thai aristocracy, with the king serving a ceremonial role. The king led the country in spiritual matters and was considered a *bodhisattva* – a spiritually superior being tasked with preserving Buddhism and aiding his subjects to achieve nirvana. Over time the kingdom reasserted Thai control over important trade networks and tributary kingdoms, bringing a wealth of luxury goods into Bangkok and spurring a literary florescence.

General
Duration 1782–1932
Language Thai (Kra-Dai)
Preceded by Ayutthaya kingdom
Succeeded by Military junta period (Thailand)

Territory
Total area (km²) 513,000

People
Population 1–3m in 1800; 4–5m in 1850
Largest city 50,000–10,000 (Rattanakosin [Bangkok])
Standing army 20,000–60,000

Social scale

Settlement hierarchy 1. Capital (Rattanakosin); 2. Great cities (*mahanakhon*); 3. Villages; 4. Hamlets.

Administrative hierarchy 1. King; 2. Cabinet ministers; 3. Provincial governors; 4. Lesser administrators.

Institutions

Legal code Three Seals Law, established in 1805.

Bureaucracy Mixed. Mostly in the hands of the aristocracy, though King Chulalongkorn attempted to create a centralised system.

Religious validation of rule Depended on "ties of incarnation" with great lineage of Buddha-like figures stretching back in time.

Property rights Mixed. In theory, all land was the property of the king, but in practice his usufructuaries had a full set of rights over the land they rented, including the right to sell it.

Price controls No data

Banking regulations Absent until the establishment of the first bank in 1888.

Economy

Taxation State used tax farms to collect revenue on drugs, spirits and trade; a land tax formed a significant proportion of state tax receipts.

Coinage Pot-duang, known in the West as "bullet coins".

Credit Unclear. The merchant industry was dominated by the large Chinese community who were probably responsible for the majority of loans.

Agricultural practices

Main crop Rice

Irrigation Present

Fertilising Absent until mid-19th century. Introduced by French authorities in region.

Cropping system Irrigated and dryland farming

Metallurgy
Base metals Bronze, iron and steel

Military equipment
Handheld weapons Swords, daggers, pikes and spears
Armour Helmets and shields
Projectiles Muskets, crossbows and simple bows
Incendiaries Use of gunpowder suggests that incendiaries were likely.
Long walls Not known to have been built.

Well-being
Life expectancy No data
Average adult stature 157 cm (male)
Irrigation & drinking water Mixed. *Muang fai* irrigation used on small
    rivers; dams of bamboo and wood channelled water through
    canals with gates used to control the flow; "luk" river-current
    powered bamboo water wheel; technology for providing
    drinking water supply existed but it is unclear whether it was
    used.
Health care Absent. No state health-care service.
Alimentary support Absent. No state alimentary support system.
Famine relief Absent. No state famine relief system.

(In)equalities
Social mobility Hereditary elite
Occupational mobility Limited
Gender equality Lower- and middle-class women had the right to
    choose husbands, but women from the upper classes had few
    rights and were under the legal authority of their husbands or
    fathers; religious ordainment was reserved for men.

Slavery Over half the population was enslaved; war captives were the most numerous type of slave; parents could sell their children to pay debts. Slavery was abolished in 1905.

Human sacrifice Absent. Forbidden by Buddhism.

Religion

Majority religious practice Theravada Buddhism

China: Hmong peoples

The Hmong are several distinct cultures who have lived for about 2,000 years in farming villages in the defensible mountains of southeast China. These villages have cooperated at times, for instance in opposition to Chinese authorities, but the lack of formal collaborative institutions often led to fragmentation. Throughout most of Hmong history, the Chinese government imposed control indirectly through native headmen known as *tusi* who were responsible for policing, tax collection and organising *corvée* labour. After Mao's revolution, however, the Hmong were aggressively incorporated into the People's Republic. "Miao", a derogatory term for the Hmong, is currently a recognised minority group in the People's Republic of China.

General
Duration 1701–1895
Language Hmong-Mien (Sino-Tibetan)
Preceded by Early Hmong settlements
Succeeded by People's Republic of China

Territory
Total area (km²) Unclear. The region under consideration extends to about 10,000 km², but the size of autonomous political units within it in the period under consideration remains unclear.

People
Population Unclear. According to some sources, there were Hmong groups that reached a population of 200,000 at this time, but it

is unclear whether this was similar, lower or higher than other groups.

Largest city 5,000–10,000. Estimated population of a large Hmong village.

Standing army 5,000. No standing army; this is a maximum estimate for the size of armed groups the Hmong might have been able to mobilise at times of rebellion against the Chinese state.

Social scale

Settlement hierarchy 1. Villages; 2. Hamlets.

Administrative hierarchy 1. Intermediary with Chinese state (*tusi*); 2. Lineage leaders; 3. Village headmen.

Institutions

Legal code Absent

Bureaucracy Absent

Religious or other validation of rule Certain individuals were considered informal leaders based on their advanced age or profound knowledge, for example of ritual matters.

Property rights Most Hmong were smallholders at this time.

Price controls No data

Banking regulations No data

Economy

Taxation Mixed. There was no local/indigenous tax system, but Chinese-appointed Hmong officials collected taxes on behalf of the Chinese state.

Coinage Absent, though some coins produced by the Qing dynasty circulated in the region.

Credit Absent

Agricultural practices

Main crops Rice and tubers

Irrigation Present
Fertilising Present
Cropping system Swidden farming

Metallurgy
Base metal Iron

Military equipment
Handheld weapons Spears and swords
Armour Rattan-cane helmets, wooden shields, body armour made
out of hide or wool, and iron limb protection.
Projectiles Firearms, eg muskets
Incendiaries Not known to have been used.
Long walls Not known to have been built.

Well-being
Life expectancy No data
Average adult stature No data
Irrigation & drinking water Hmong groups who practised wet rice
terrace irrigation used the horse-driven wooden water-wheel;
drinking water came from wells and springs.
Health care Absent. No Hmong state to provide centralised health-
care system; medical services provided by ritual specialists.
Alimentary support Absent. No Hmong state to provide a centralised
system of alimentary support.
Famine relief Absent. No Hmong state to provide a centralised
system of famine relief.

(In)equalities
Social mobility Absent. Very little social stratification.
Occupational mobility Absent. Most Hmong were subsistence
farmers.
Gender equality Gender-based division of labour; both men and

women could in theory act as informal leaders, but in practice these positions were usually filled by men.

Slavery Probably absent

Human sacrifice Absent

Religion

Majority religious practices Hmong religion. Shamanism; animism; ancestor worship.

Turkey: Ottoman Empire

After conquering the Ottoman Emirate, Timur (also known as Tamerlane) focused his attention on the Persian heartland, allowing the Ottomans to reclaim much of their lost territory throughout Turkey and the Balkans. The *coup de grâce* came in 1453 CE when Sultan Mehmet II seized Constantinople from the Byzantines. Along with the Silk Road trade routes, Mehmet took from the defeated Roman Empire the ancient honorific Caesar, adding his own grandiose title "ruler of the two continents and the two seas". By the 16th century, Ottomans held sway over lands stretching from modern-day Morocco to the west, Yemen to the south, Iraq to the east and Czechia to the north.

General
Duration 1413–1922
Languages Turkish (Turkic); Arabic (Afro-Asiatic); Persian (Indo-European); other languages indigenous to provincial populations.
Preceded by Timurid Empire
Succeeded by Modern Turkey

Territory
Total area (km²) 522,000 in 1421 CE; 2.3m in 1500; 4.8m in 1600; 5.2m in 1680; 4.9m in 1700.

People
Population 5m in 1421 CE; 9m in 1500; 28m in 1600; 24m in 1700; 24m in 1800; 25m in 1900.

Largest city 200,000–410,000 in 1500 CE; 650,000–700,000 in 1600; 700,000 in 1700; 570,000 in 1800; 1.125m in 1914 (Istanbul).

Standing army 50,000–90,000 in 1500 CE; 100,000–200,000 in 1600

Social scale

Settlement hierarchy 1. Capital (Istanbul); 2. Provincial centres; 3. District centres; 4. Towns; 5. Villages; 6. Nomadic camps.

Administrative hierarchy 1. Sultan; 2. Grand Vizier; 3. Imperial Council; 4. Imperial Treasury; 5. Provincial governors; 6. Treasurers (*defterdar*); 7. Provincial council; 8. Lesser provincial administration; 9. City/town judges.

Institutions

Legal code Secular law (*kanun*) and religious law (*shari'a*).

Bureaucracy Bureaucracy. Recruited from the ranks of enslaved people.

Religious validation of rule Ruler was believed to be divinely appointed.

Property rights Limited amount of private ownership of land.

Price controls Price ceilings (*narh*) set, but unclear whether they were either enforced or followed.

Banking regulations Formal banks first established in the 19th century. The state regulated banking based on its interpretation of the Hanafi school of Islamic jurisprudence.

Economy

Taxation Tax on agricultural production; *jizya* (head tax collection from non-Muslims); *za'kat* (charity) tax; trade tax.

Coinage Gold *sultani* and silver *akce*.

Credit Ottoman law allowed for a wide range of credit arrangements, including interest-bearing loans.

Agricultural practices
Main crop Wheat
Irrigation Present
Fertilising Present
Cropping system Modern mechanical agriculture in the 19th century

Metallurgy
Base metals Bronze, iron and steel

Military equipment
Handheld weapons Sabres, spears, daggers, maces and battle axes
Armour Moorish leather shields; heavy cavalry wore helmets, limb
    armour and chain mail; plate cuirasses also used for body
    armour.
Projectiles Muskets, pistols and field cannon
Incendiaries Grenades
Long walls Not known to have been built.

Well-being
Life expectancy 35 years from birth
Average adult stature 165 cm (male) in the immediately succeeding
    period (1840–1910).
Irrigation & drinking water Irrigation systems in Egypt rebuilt; water
    sent to cities through aqueducts.
Health care Absent. State began to provide welfare services only in
    the 19th century; however, there were already 90 hospitals across
    the empire by the end of the 16th century.
Alimentary support Absent. State began to provide welfare services
    only in the 19th century; till then, alimentary support provided
    by private donors.
Famine relief Food moved from surplus areas to famine areas; price
    fixing, tax breaks/adjustments; granary system designed to
    ensure consistent supply of grain to the capital.

(In)equalities

Social mobility Hereditary elite

Occupational mobility Limited

Gender equality Only a minority of wealthy elite women could achieve a measure of power and influence; however, commoner women were often important family wage-earners in a variety of occupations.

Slavery Chattel slavery.

Human sacrifice Absent. Forbidden by Islam.

Religion

Majority religious practice Sunni Islam

Spain: Habsburg Empire

Following the deaths of both his grandfathers, Ferdinand II of Aragon in 1516 CE and the Holy Roman Emperor Maximilian I in 1519, Charles V, a Habsburg on his maternal side, became the ruler of a vast array of territories in Spain, the Holy Roman Empire, Low Countries, Italy and the Americas. Spain's additional territorial conquests (which also included the Philippines in Asia) made it the first "empire on which the sun never sets" and brought in wealth from around the world, which led to a rapid urbanisation and marketisation, as Spanish imperial cities became major manufacturing centres. Spanish law was based on Catholic doctrine and was nominally enforced throughout the empire, but with stark differences in rights and privileges of subjects based on class, ethnicity, gender and social status.

General

Duration 1516–1700

Languages Spanish (Indo-European); Italian, French, Flemish, German (Indo-European); indigenous languages (eg Quechua, Aymara, Mayan, Nahuatl).

Preceded by Kingdom of Castile; kingdom of Aragon

Succeeded by Bourbon Spain

Territory

Total area (km²) 5m in 1610; 10m in 1700

People

Population 29m in 1550

Largest city 224,000 in Naples (1600)

Standing army 300,000 in 1630

Social scale

Settlement hierarchy 1. Capital (Madrid); 2. Regional capitals (Barcelona, Seville, Zaragoza and Pamplona); 3. Major cities (eg Toledo); 4. Towns; 5. Villages.

Administrative hierarchy 1. King; 2. Grand Chancellor; 3. Chief Council Secretaries; 4. Viceroys or military governors; 5. Provincial and colonial councils; 6. Provincial and colonial bureaucracies; 7. Local lords; 8. Village administrations.

Institutions

Legal code Roman and Spanish law

Bureaucracy Composed of the aristocracy, though sometimes those of common status held bureaucratic positions.

Religious validation of rule Hereditary monarchy. Legitimating ideology founded on medieval Christian notions that social hierarchies reflected the heavenly order.

Property rights Present

Price controls The issue of 20 million ducats' worth of copper coins in 1621–26 resulted in unprecedented inflation, which the monarchy attempted to ameliorate through price controls; however, this measure failed.

Banking regulations Unclear

Economy

Taxation Decentralised taxation system fragmented into several local tax-raising authorities with considerable opportunities to shape rates, incidence and collection.

Coinage Gold, silver and copper

Credit Present

Agricultural practices
Main crops Wheat in the European territories; maize and rice in
    colonial territories.
Irrigation Present
Fertilising Present
Cropping system Crop rotation

Metallurgy
Base metals Bronze, iron and steel

Military equipment
Handheld weapons Daggers, swords, pikes, lances and polearms
Armour Captains and wealthier nobles wore three-quarter armour
    (helmet, breastplate and limb protection); colonial troops
    adopted indigenous quilted cotton armour, which was more
    comfortable in the New World's humid climate.
Projectiles Arquebuses, muskets and cannon
Incendiaries Siege artillery
Long walls Not known to have been built.

Well-being
Life expectancy No data
Average adult stature No data
Irrigation & drinking water No systemic nationwide irrigation
    programmes, but Iberian cities and towns received drinking
    water from aqueducts and underground pipe networks.
Health care In the Iberian peninsula, many cities boasted hospitals
    supported by groups such as guilds, lay confraternities, royal
    officials and convents; hospitals were established in the colonies
    as well, along with the *leprosaria* seen in most provincial
    capitals. Most health-care services were run by the church.
Alimentary support Limited. Mostly provided by female convents
    and through hospitals.

Famine relief Present. For example, in the early 17th century, the Spanish Crown regulated the price of rice in the Philippines to combat the effects of widespread famine, though to little effect.

(In)equalities

Social mobility Limited. Largely depended on birth, and "racial purity" in particular was a prerequisite for elite status across the empire; indeed, a rigid social hierarchy gradually formed based on legally defined racial categories.

Occupational mobility Likely to have been low, given rigid social hierarchies.

Gender equality Christian ideology fostered significant gender inequality. However, women could inherit property, though within certain limitations.

Slavery Practised across the colonies; due to the decimation of the native population as a result of violent colonial oppression and disease, they were mostly replaced with enslaved people from Africa.

Human sacrifice Absent. Forbidden by Christianity.

Religion

Majority religious practice Roman Catholicism

Modern: 1800 to 2000 CE

Great Britain: Second British Empire

The Second British Empire began after the loss of the First Empire's most populous colony, the United States. Even without this productive territory, the empire was vast. At home, continuing secularisation gave elected members of parliament increased influence at the expense of the crown. Abroad, Britain's military operations saw it ever more deeply involved in the lives of its subjects, as new taxes were levied, old ones increased and resource extraction expanded to supply the empire. The British conferred sharply different rights on their (white) British citizens and their non-British peoples, and the racially motivated distinction between "citizen" and "dependent" colonies accounts in large part for their divergent post-colonial experiences.

General
Duration 1783–1914
Languages English (Indo-European); Hindi (Indo-European); Punjabi (Indo-European); Bengali (Indo-European); other indigenous languages.
Preceded by First British Empire. The First British Empire was largely made up of Great Britain's North American colonies; after most of these became independent in 1783, the Second British Empire extended across Asia, the Pacific, Canada and Africa.
Succeeded by Wartime Britain

Territory
Total area (km²) 26m in 1800; 35.5m in 1900

People
Population 107m in 1800; 410m in 1900
Largest city 900,000 in 1800; 6.5m in 1900 (London)
Standing army 250,000 in 1900

Social scale
Settlement hierarchy 1. Capital (London); 2. Colonial capitals
(eg Calcutta); 3. Major cities (eg Manchester, Delhi, Dublin);
4. Lesser cities; 5. Towns; 6. Villages.
Administrative hierarchy 1. Monarch; 2. Parliament; 3. UK regional
administrative units, governors, colonial officers and secretaries;
4. Colonial councils (eg Indian Civil Service); 5. Bureaucratic
officials; 6. Colonial indigenous officials; 7. Lesser officers.

Institutions
Legal code English common and statutory law, amended with
colonial statutes wherever deemed necessary.
Bureaucracy In Britain, expanding system of full-time salaried
bureaucrats; in India, a system of (mostly non-native) salaried
officials known as the Indian Civil Service, introduced in 1858.
Religious or other validation of rule Hereditary rule, with democratic
elements. Monarch inherited title by blood; members of
parliament elected democratically, though throughout this
period voting was restricted to relatively wealthy adult men.
Property rights Besides gender, ownership of private property was
the main criterion for determining a person's right to vote.
Price controls Present. For example, between 1815 and 1846, the Corn
Laws raised the price of food and grain imported to Britain in
order to favour domestic producers; they were repealed as a

result of the Irish famine, resulting in a shift towards liberalised
trade.

Banking regulations Through the Bank Charter Act of 1844,
Parliament restricted the powers of British banks and endowed
the central Bank of England with the power to issue notes; the
following year the Act was extended to Ireland.

Economy

Taxation By the early 20th century, the bulk of colonial expenditure
was funded by revenue raised in the colonies themselves; the
colonial government also used taxation to favour certain
industries over others.

Coinage Gold sterling in Britain and non-American self-governing
colonies; silver rupees in India, Ceylon, British East Africa and
Indian Ocean territories; silver dollars in Malaya; bronze
manillas, cowrie shells and other traditional exchange devices in
remaining African territories.

Credit Present

Agricultural practices

Main crops Wheat. Rice and sugar in parts of the empire
Irrigation Present
Fertilising Present
Cropping system Modern mechanised agriculture

Metallurgy

Base metals Steel, iron and brass

Military equipment

Handheld weapons Bayonets; cavalrymen used swords and lances.
Armour Helmets and leg protection
Projectiles Rifles, muskets and cannon; pistols from the 1850s
onwards.

Incendiaries Siege artillery

Long walls Not known to have been built.

Well-being

Life expectancy 40 years from birth (male; England); 42 years (female; England). Life expectancy probably varied significantly based on class, and was different in the colonies; eg male life expectancy in Canada and the USA during this period was 39 years. Detailed records are lacking for other regions.

Average adult stature 170 cm (male; England); 156 cm (female; England). Average stature may have been different in the colonies; however, at this time male stature was 170 cm in Canada and 173 cm in the USA.

Irrigation & drinking water From the 1840s onwards, a water supply system known as the "gravitation scheme" (involving damming rivers, raising lakes, and/or flooding valleys and then piping the water to cities) was introduced to major cities across Britain as well as to colonial cities such as Bombay, Colombo, Hong Kong and Singapore; new irrigation systems were introduced, for example, in India and Egypt.

Health care Absent. Before 1900, largely provided by charities, Poor Law committees and the private sector. Centralised National Health Service established in 1948.

Alimentary support In Britain, the 1834 Poor Law established that the poor could only receive alimentary support in exchange for several hours' hard work every day in specially constructed workhouses.

Famine relief Absent. Both Ireland and India (eg 1866, 1869, 1874, 1876–78, etc.) suffered catastrophic famines at this time, but the British government provided no state-sponsored support, arguing that famines were a corrective for overpopulation.

(In)equalities

Social mobility Relatively high social mobility in Britain, with significant expansion of the middle classes.

Occupational mobility Relatively high intergenerational occupational mobility in Britain.

Gender equality Victorian ideology enforced marked gender inequality and rigid gender roles.

Slavery Mixed. Parliament abolished the slave trade throughout the British Empire in 1807, but slavery itself persisted in the colonies until it was definitively abolished in 1838.

Human sacrifice Absent. Forbidden by Christianity.

Religion

Majority religious practices Anglican Christianity; Hinduism; Sikhism; Roman Catholic Christianity; Jainism; indigenous Pacific religions; indigenous African religions.

USA: Antebellum America

The Paris Peace Treaty of 1783 confirmed the American Continental Army's victory over the British, but the United States of America was left with enormous war debts. To gain resources, the new nation pursued a policy of "Manifest Destiny", arguing that the continent belonged by right to white, Christian settlers. The ensuing influx of migrants, along with major disease outbreaks and the violent expansionist tactics of the US government, led to the deaths of 90% of the indigenous populations in some territories. Conflicts over whether to foster an industrial or agrarian economy, and therefore whether to extend or abolish slavery, culminated in the civil war.

General
Duration 1776–1861
Languages English (Indo-European); indigenous languages
    (eg Iroquoian languages).
Preceded by British Empire
Succeeded by American civil war and Reconstruction eras

Territory
Total area (km²) 2.2m in 1790; 4.5m in 1820; 8.1m in 1860

People
Population 3.9m in 1790; 9.6m in 1820; 31.4m in 1860
Largest city 33,000 in 1790; 120,000 in 1820; 810,000 in 1860 (New
    York).
Standing army 6,000–7,000. Expanded to 115,000 during the
    Mexican war.

Social scale

Settlement hierarchy 1. Capital (Washington DC since 1802); 2. Other
major cities (eg Philadelphia, New York); 3. State capitals;
4. County centres; 5. Townships. Before 1802, Congress met in
various places in Philadelphia and New York.

Administrative hierarchy 1. President; 2. Congress (Senate and House
of Representatives); 3. State governors; 4. State legislatures;
5. Mayors; 6. Town/city boards.

Institutions

Legal code US Constitution

Bureaucracy Divided into executive, legislative and judiciary
branches; a professionalised, national-level, neutral bureaucracy
began to emerge in the 1880s.

Religious or other validation of rule Democratic republic. President
elected through democratic vote.

Property rights Free citizens had the right to own private property
but the state governments had broad powers to regulate property
use.

Price controls Absent. First experiments with price controls in the US
took place during the second world war.

Banking regulations State-managed National Bank established on
Alexander Hamilton's initiative in 1791, but abolished/
re-established throughout the period. Wide range of banking
regulations established by individual states, including highly
regulated private banks in New York, Ohio and Michigan.

Economy

Taxation Taxes had been a key cause of the revolutionary war, so the
US government rarely and reluctantly imposed direct taxes and
excises; majority of state revenues derived from tariffs.

Coinage Dollars; gold and silver coins. The Constitution established that only the central government had the right to mint coins, issue paper money and generally regulate currency. A typical wage during this period was $1 per day. The value of money fluctuated, with a bushel of wheat costing between $1 and $2, though the country experienced high inflation in the run-up to the civil war.

Credit Most Americans preferred banknotes to bills of credit, as they were legal tender and could be converted into gold or silver at predetermined rates.

Agricultural practices
Main crops Wheat and maize
Irrigation Present
Fertilising Present
Cropping system Modern mechanised agriculture

Metallurgy
Base metals Bronze, iron and steel

Military equipment
Handheld weapons Swords were the traditional weapon of cavalry and officers until 1830; after 1830, they were gradually replaced by handguns.

Armour Not known to have been widely used.

Projectiles Rifles, carbines, muskets, cannon, pistols and bayonets; handguns became the weapons of choice for much of the army after the invention of the Colt Paterson revolver in 1836.

Incendiaries Siege artillery

Long walls Not known to have been built.

Well-being
Life expectancy Life expectancy after reaching the age of 10 declined from 55 in 1800 to 48 in 1855.

Irrigation & drinking water Throughout the 19th century, starting in
1799, cities gradually shifted from local water sources to
centralised water systems; irrigation was essential to agriculture.

Health care Absent. No state-managed health-care system or
services.

Alimentary support Absent. Until 1935, the poor could only hope to
benefit from the Poor Laws, which were administered by local
authorities and allowed for the provision of minimal aid to
those deemed "worthy" or "deserving".

Famine relief None. No famines recorded for this time period.

(In)equalities

Social mobility Relatively high social mobility compared with
contemporary European societies, particularly with regard to
unskilled workers moving from working class to lower middle
class and skilled workers becoming wealthy entrepreneurs.

Occupational mobility Relatively high occupational mobility
compared with contemporary European societies.

Gender equality Conservative ideological notions such as
"republican motherhood" fostered gender inequality by
assigning rigid roles to each gender; the movement for women's
rights may be said to have begun either in the 1830s, with Sarah
and Angelina Grimké, or with the 1848 Seneca Falls convention.

Slavery Economy founded on the labour of enslaved Africans, their
descendants, and Native Americans; slavery as an institution
was rooted in white supremacist ideology.

Human sacrifice Absent. Forbidden by Christianity.

Religion

Majority religious practices Anglican Christianity; Roman Catholic
Christianity; indigenous North American religions.

Germany: Third Reich

Germany was devastated by the first world war, burdened by famine, destruction and indemnities owed to the victors. The new Weimar Republic tried to rebuild the country, but the Great Depression fuelled a surge of nationalist fervour culminating in the election of the Nationalist Socialist Party, or "Nazis", in 1932. Adolf Hitler became chancellor the following year and quickly dismantled democratic institutions to establish a totalitarian dictatorship. The Nazis labelled their regime the Third Reich and offered distorted logic to support claims that a homogenous "German" culture and race was the rightful leader of the world. Their genocidal policies killed 6 million Jews and 11 million other people deemed "undesirable".

General
Duration 1933–45
Language German (Indo-European)
Preceded by Weimar Republic
Succeeded by Occupied West and East Germany

Territory
Total area (km²) 468,800 in 1933; 583,400 in 1939; 353,460 in 1946

People
Population 65.3m in 1933; 65.1m in 1946
Largest city 4m (Berlin, 1930)
Standing army 4.722m in 1939; 11m in 1943; 9.7m in 1945

Social scale
Settlement hierarchy 1. Capital (Berlin); 2. Major (Führer) cities (Linz,

Munich, Nuremberg and Hamburg); 3. Lesser cities; 4. Towns;
5. Villages.

Administrative hierarchy 1. Führer; 2. Führer-appointed chief
ministers; 3. Agencies and ministries founded or re-shaped by
chief ministers; 4. Provincial governors; 5. Provincial
administration; 6. Local administration.

Institutions

Legal code The 1919 Weimar constitution was never officially
repealed; however, Hitler and the Nazi government generally
took a cavalier approach to it.

Bureaucracy Hitler frequently established new offices and agencies
without specifying clear lines of demarcation of responsibility
with existing government entities; the result was a chaotic,
inefficient bureaucracy plagued by internal rivalries.

Religious or other validation of rule Fascist ideology. Basis of Hitler's
authority was not the constitution, but his direct relationship
with the German nation, and the belief that it was his destiny to
lead it and restore its supposed past greatness.

Property rights Present

Price controls Throughout the 1930s, the Nazi regime attempted to
stimulate production while maintaining price stability.

Banking regulations Regulatory frameworks established in 1934 for
key business sectors, including banking.

Economy

Taxation Beginning in 1937, confiscation of property owned by
Jewish citizens was also used to refinance the national debt.

Coinage Reichsmark (RM); 0.56 RM per 4 lb of bread. In 1937 average
wages were 1,030 RM (agriculture); 1,871 RM (industry); 2,356 RM
(services excluding military).

Credit State-regulated banks issued large loans to private business to
  stimulate industrial development.

Agricultural practices
Main crop Wheat
Irrigation Present
Fertilising Present
Cropping system Modern mechanised agriculture

Metallurgy
Base metals Steel and iron

Military equipment
Handheld weapons Combat knives
Armour Helmets
Projectiles Pistols, rifles, submachine guns, flame-throwers,
  machine guns, anti-tank and anti-aircraft guns.
Incendiaries Grenades, siege artillery
Long walls Not known to have been built.

Well-being
Life expectancy 60–65 years from birth (German citizens)
Average adult stature 174 cm (male; German citizens)
Irrigation & drinking water Mixed. Agriculture largely rain-fed;
  drinking water and water diversion projects present.
Health care In 1933, the state inaugurated an extensive eugenics
  programme, including policies authorising forced abortion,
  sterilisation and euthanasia of people deemed undesirable in
  one way or another.
Alimentary support State provided supplementary food to larger
  families.
Famine relief Mixed. No major famines within the Third Reich itself;

however, rationing was introduced at the start of the first world
war and Germans experienced chronic food shortages after 1944.

(In)equalities

Social mobility Mixed. Social mobility was largely confined to
members of the Nazi party; several groups – defined on the basis
of race, sexual orientation and beliefs – suffered downward
mobility and outright persecution.

Occupational mobility Mixed. Probably reflected trends in social
mobility.

Gender equality Entrenched gender inequality, with women largely
seen as instruments for the reproduction of the Aryan race.
State-sponsored oppression of gay men.

Slavery Present

Human sacrifice Absent. Forbidden by Christianity and Judaism.

Religion

Majority religious practices Lutheran Christianity; Roman
Catholicism; Judaism.

Russia: USSR

In 1917, mass protests against food rationing brought down Russia's Tsarist regime. The Communist Party of the Soviet Union (CPSU) under Vladimir Lenin seized control of the empire, establishing the Union of Soviet Socialist Republics (USSR) in 1922. The new constitution sought to redistribute wealth evenly, but concentrated power in the party's *Politburo*. After Lenin died, Joseph Stalin took power, purging dissenters and pursuing centrally planned industrialisation and collectivisation. The government liberalised a little after Stalin's death in 1953 and citizens enjoyed fairly high levels of well-being. However, when the price of oil plummeted in the 1980s, Russia's stagnant economy could not recover and in 1992 the USSR collapsed.

General
Duration 1917–89
Language Russian (Indo-European)
Preceded by Russian Empire
Succeeded by Russian Federation

Territory
Total area (km²) 2.16m in 1920; 2.17m in 1930; 2.18m in 1940; 2.23m in 1950; 2.1m in 1960; 1.97m in 1970; 1.84m in 1980; 1.71m in 1990.

People
Population 147m in 1926; 162m in 1937; 209m in 1956; 242m in 1970; 262m in 1979; 287m in 1989.
Largest city 1.764m in 1930; 5.1m in 1950; 9.8m in 1970 (Moscow)

Standing army 5m in 1922. Numbers oscillated throughout the
decades but repeatedly returned to a figure of c. 5m: in 1922, at
the eve of the second world war, and between 1970 and 1990.

Social scale

Settlement hierarchy 1. Capital (Moscow); 2. Other large cities (eg
Leningrad); 3. Capitals of the Union Republics; 4. Major towns;
5. Lesser towns; 6. Villages.

Administrative hierarchy 1. Politburo; 2. Central CPSU Committee;
3. Regional (*oblast*) CPSU committee; 4. District (*raion*) CPSU
committee, 5. Local CPSU committee.

Institutions

Legal code Pre-revolutionary legal code abolished during Revolution;
replaced with civil code based on western European civil law in
the 1920s; Soviet law subsequently became mainly an
instrument for the implementation of party policy and national
economic planning.

Bureaucracy Centralised bureaucracy made up of hundreds of
thousands of full-time, paid officials belonging to the CPSU.

Religious or other validation of rule Ruler was elected by Communist
Party delegates.

Property rights Soviet law distinguished between socialist property
(ie state-owned and collective or cooperative property) and
individually owned private property (ie consumer goods, cars,
houses and agricultural equipment for private farming).

Price controls The state raised food prices in 1961–62, resulting in
widespread protest; though these protests were quelled, the state
never again raised food prices.

Banking regulations Banks were controlled by the state.

Economy

Taxation Present

Coinage Roubles.

Credit Largely absent. State bank was largely used for savings and making payments rather than issuing credit.

Agricultural practices

Main crops Wheat, rye, rice

Irrigation Present

Fertilising Present

Cropping system Modern mechanised agriculture

Metallurgy

Base metals Steel and iron

Military equipment

Handheld weapons Combat knives and bayonets

Armour Helmets and breastplates. The SN-42 breastplate consisted of two pressed steel plates designed to protect torso and groin. "SN" is an acronym for Stalnoi Nagrudnik ("steel breastplate") and "42" indicated the year it was invented. Because of its weight, it was mostly worn by assault engineers rather than infantry fighting in the open.

Projectiles Pistols, rifles, submachine guns, machine guns, rocket launchers, anti-tank and anti-aircraft guns.

Incendiaries Grenades and anti-tank incendiaries (eg Zuckerman's bottle-thrower), siege artillery.

Long walls USSR had the world's longest land border which was heavily fortified and guarded by dedicated border troops. The Berlin Wall was a tangible, physical symbol of the cold war and there were a number of other border fortification systems separating NATO countries from Warsaw Pact countries in Europe.

Well-being

Life expectancy In 1940: 44 years from birth (male), 49 years
(female); in 1960: 64 years from birth (male), 71 years (female);
in 1990: 65 years from birth (male), 74 years (female).

Average adult stature In 1950: 173 cm (male), 161 cm (female); in
1980: 177 cm (male), 164 cm (female).

Irrigation & drinking water Soviet state completed major irrigation
and water-diversion projects.

Health care By the 1960s, most citizens were able to benefit from
state-funded health care.

Alimentary support The state instituted a centralised resource
distribution system from the start, but overall it was inefficient
(and destructive c. 1918–49) and most people relied on *blat*
("favours") for basic goods, including food.

Famine relief Between 1917 and 1949, the USSR was in a near-
constant state of famine, due partly to wars and partly to policies
such as the forced requisition of grain, though these measures
were briefly relaxed in 1925–28. The situation improved
considerably from the 1950s onwards, but many people relied on
blat instead of the state to obtain basic resources.

(In)equalities

Social mobility High social mobility at the beginning of the period;
however, opportunities were largely constrained by class
background.

Occupational mobility Present

Gender equality In the 1920s, women's property and inheritance
rights were made equal to men's, abortion was available on
demand and divorce was made easier. Eventually, however,
abortion was outlawed again, divorce made more difficult and
inheritance rights confined to the offspring of registered

marriages. Women were expected to take care of domestic duties but also seek employment ("double burden").

Slavery Absent. Chattel slavery was non-existent, though millions of labour-camp inmates lacked enforceable legal rights.

Human sacrifice Absent

Religion

Majority religious practice Marxism–Leninism was the official state ideology; other religious practices were suppressed by Soviet state, with churches closed and priests arrested.

Rankings

10 largest societies by territory: ancient

Total approximate area under the society's authority at its greatest extent

Society	Approx. extent (km²)	Region
1 Eastern Han Empire	6.5m	East Asia
2 Roman Principate	5.8m	Europe
3 Achaemenid Empire	5.5m	Southwest Asia
4 Alexander the Great's Empire	5.2m	Europe
5 Western Han Empire	4.9m	East Asia
6 Western Jin dynasty	4.5m	East Asia
7 Roman Dominate	4–4.5m	Europe
8 Xianbei confederacy	2.3–4.5m	Central Asia
9 Xiongnu confederacy	4.2m	Central Asia
10 Mauryan Empire	4m	South Asia

10 largest societies by territory: medieval

Total approximate area under the society's authority at its greatest extent

Society	Approx. extent (km²)	Region
1 Mongolian Empire	25m	Central Asia
2 Yuan dynasty	11–24m	East Asia
3 Umayyad caliphate	9–11m	Southwest Asia
4 Abbasid caliphate	8.3m	Southwest Asia
5 Göktürk khanate	4.5–7.5m	Central Asia
6 Rashidun caliphate	6.4m	Southwest Asia
7 Tang dynasty	6.225m	East Asia
8 Golden Horde khanate	6m	Europe and Central Asia
9 Timurid Empire	5.5m	Central Asia
10 Tibetan Empire	4.6m	Central Asia

10 largest societies by territory: early modern

Total approximate area under the society's authority at its greatest extent

	Society	Approx. extent (km²)	Region
1	First British Empire	24.5m	Europe
2	Russian Empire	22.8m	Europe
3	Qing dynasty	13.1m	East Asia
4	French Colonial Empire	11.5m	Europe
5	Habsburg Spanish Empire	10m	Europe
6	Iberian Union	7m	Europe
7	Ottoman Empire	5.2m	West Asia
8	Mughal Empire	3.2–4.5m	South Asia
9	Bourbon kingdom	2.5–3m	Europe
10	Safavid Emirate	2.7m	Southwest Asia

10 largest societies by territory in the entire preindustrial era

Total approximate area under the society's authority at its greatest extent

	Society	Approx. extent (km²)	Region	Period
1	Mongolian Empire	25m	Central Asia	Medieval
2	First British Empire	24.5m	Europe	Early Modern
3	Yuan dynasty	11–24m	East Asia	Medieval
4	Russian Empire	22.8m	Europe	Early Modern
5	Qing dynasty	13.1m	East Asia	Early Modern
6	French Colonial Empire	11.5m	Europe	Early Modern
7	Umayyad caliphate	9–11m	Southwest Asia	Medieval
8	Habsburg Spanish Empire	10m	Europe	Early Modern
9	Abbasid caliphate	8.3m	Southwest Asia	Medieval
10	Göktürk khanate	4.5–7.5m	Central Asia	Medieval

10 most populous societies: ancient

Greatest total approximate population living in society territory

	Society	Approx. population	Region
1	Mauryan Empire	20–100m	South Asia
2	Roman Dominate	40–70m	Europe
3	Roman Principate	50–60m	Europe
4	Western Han	57.6m	East Asia
5	Eastern Han Empire	48–50m	East Asia
6	Qin Empire	40m	East Asia
7	Northern Wei dynasty	32m	East Asia
8	Hephthalite kingdom	26.5m	Central Asia
9	Late Roman Republic	25–35m	Europe
10	Achaemenid Empire	20–26m	Southwest Asia

10 most populous societies: medieval

Greatest total approximate population living in society territory

	Society	Approx. population	Region
1	Ming dynasty	90–110m	East Asia
2	Northern Song dynasty	60–100m	East Asia
3	Yuan dynasty	60.5–85m	East Asia
4	Tang dynasty	60–80m	East Asia
5	Later Jin dynasty	45–54m	East Asia
6	Timurid Empire	49m	Central Asia
7	Sui dynasty	46m	East Asia
8	Vijayanagara Empire	25m	South Asia
=9	Abbasid caliphate	23–33m	Southwest Asia
=9	Umayyad caliphate	23–33m	Southwest Asia

10 most populous societies: early modern

Greatest total approximate population living in society territory

	Society	Approx. population	Region
1	Qing dynasty	334–348m	East Asia
2	First British Empire	200–250m	Europe
3	Mughal Empire	110–150m	South Asia
4	French Colonial Empire	30–40m	Europe
5	Tokugawa Shogunate	29–32m	East Asia
6	Iberian Union	30m	Europe
7	Habsburg Spanish Empire	29m	Europe
8	Russian Empire	20–35m	Europe
9	Bourbon kingdom	28.5m	Europe
10	Ottoman Empire	28m	West Asia

10 most populous societies in the entire preindustrial era

Greatest total approximate population living in society territory

	Society	Approx. population	Region	Period
1	Qing dynasty	334–348m	East Asia	Early Modern
2	First British Empire	200–250m	Europe	Early Modern
3	Mughal Empire	110–150m	South Asia	Early Modern
4	Ming dynasty	90–110m	East Asia	Medieval
5	Northern Song dynasty	60–100m	East Asia	Medieval
6	Yuan dynasty	60.5–85m	East Asia	Medieval
7	Tang dynasty	60–80m	East Asia	Medieval
8	Roman Dominate	40–70m	Europe	Ancient
9	Western Han	57.6–60m	East Asia	Ancient
10	Roman Principate	50–60m	Europe	Ancient

10 most populous cities: ancient

Greatest total approximate population living in an urban area

	Society	Approx. population	City	Region
1	Roman Principate	900,000–1.1m	Rome	Europe
2	Roman Dominate	800,000	Rome	Europe
=3	Western Jin dynasty	600,000	Luoyang	East Asia
=3	Northern Wei dynasty	600,000	Luoyang	East Asia
=3	Parthian Empire	600,000	Seleucia-Ctesiphon	Southwest Asia
6	Ptolemaic kingdom	500,000–600,000	Alexandria	North Africa
7	Western Roman Empire	500,000	Rome	Europe
8	Late Republican Rome	400,000	Rome	Europe
9	Western Han Empire	250,000–400,000	Chang'an	East Asia
10	Qin Empire	350,000	Linzi	East Asia

10 most populous cities: medieval

Greatest total approximate population living in an urban area

	Society	Approx. population	City	Region
=1	Tang dynasty	1m	Chang'an	East Asia
=1	Northern Song dynasty	1m	Kaifeng	East Asia
3	Angkor kingdom	750,000–1m	Angkor	Southeast Asia
4	Seljuq sultanate	500,000–1m	Baghdad	West Asia
5	Abbasid caliphate	900,000	Baghdad	Southwest Asia
6	Buyid confederation	500,000–900,000	Baghdad	Southwest Asia
7	Yuan dynasty	800,000	Hangzhou	East Asia
8	Sui dynasty	500,000	Luoyang	East Asia
9	Sassanid Empire	400,000–500,000	Ctesiphon	Southwest Asia
10	Delhi sultanate	200,000–400,000	Delhi	South Asia

10 most populous cities: early modern

Greatest total approximate population living in an urban area

	Society	Approx. population	City	Region
1	Tokugawa Shogunate	1.4m	Edo	East Asia
=2	Qing dynasty	1m	Beijing	East Asia
=2	First British Empire	1m	London	Europe
4	Ottoman Empire	700,000	Istanbul	West Asia
5	Bourbon kingdom	600,000	Paris	Europe
6	Azuchi–Momoyama period Japan	300,000	Kyoto	East Asia
7	Habsburg Spanish Empire	224,000	Naples	Europe
8	Safavid Emirate	200,000	Isfahan	Southwest Asia
9	Papal States, early modern period	158,000	Rome	Europe
10	Ayutthaya kingdom	155,000	Ayutthaya	Southeast Asia

10 most populous cities in the entire preindustrial era

Greatest total approximate population living in an urban area

	Society	Approx. population	City	Region	Period
1	Tokugawa Shogunate	1.4m	Edo	East Asia	Early Modern
=2	Qing dynasty	1m	Beijing	East Asia	Early Modern
=2	T'ang dynasty	1m	Chang'an	East Asia	Medieval
=2	Abbasid caliphate	1m	Baghdad	Southwest Asia	Medieval
=2	First British Empire	1m	London	Europe	Early Modern
6	Roman Principate	900,000–1m	Rome	Western Europe	Ancient
7	Angkor kingdom	750,000–1m	Angkor	Southeast Asia	Medieval
8	Seljuq sultanate	500,000–1m	Baghdad	Southwest Asia	Medieval
9	Buyid confederation	500,000–900,000	Baghdad	Southwest Asia	Medieval
10	Yuan dynasty	800,000	Hangzhou	East Asia	Medieval

10 largest buildings by total area: ancient

Total approximate area encompassed by monumental building

Society	Approx. extent (area m²)	Building	Region
1 Imperial Qin	600,000	Epang Hall, Qin Epang Palace at Shaanxi, China	East Asia
2 Kofun period Japan	150,000	Diasen Tumulus Burial Mound at Osaka, Japan	East Asia
3 Neo-Assyrian Empire	100,000	Palace at Nineveh, Iraq	Southwest Asia
4 Western Han Empire	80,000	Front Hall, Weiyang Palace at Chang'an, China	East Asia
5 Eastern Roman Empire	51,000	Hippodrome at Constantinople, Turkey	West Asia
6 Roman Dominate	30,000	Diocletian's Palace at Dalmatia, Croatia	Europe
7 Roman Principate	24,000	Colosseum at Rome, Italy	Europe
8 First Intermediate period Egypt	16,200	Saff-tomb of King Intef I at Thebes, Egypt	North Africa
9 Lydian kingdom	13,225	Temple of Artemis at Ephesus, Turkey	West Asia
10 Bronze Age Central Anatolia	11,000	Warshama Palace at Kütlepe, Turkey	West Asia

10 largest buildings by total area: medieval

Total approximate area encompassed by monumental building

Society	Approx. extent (area m²)	Building	Region
1 Angkor kingdom	820,000	Angkor Wat at Angkor, Cambodia	Southeast Asia
2 Tang dynasty	690,000	Eastern Palace of the Crown Prince at Taijigong Palace City, Chang'an	East Asia
3 Asuka kingdom	640,000	Imperial Palace at Fujiwara, Japan	East Asia
4 Wari Empire	470,000	Pikillacta Complex at Pikillacta, Peru	South America

10 tallest buildings: early modern

Maximum approximate height reached by tallest portion of monumental building

Society	Approx. height (m)	Building	Region
1 Capetian kingdom	153	St Pierre's Cathedral at Beauvais, France	Europe
2 Polish–Lithuanian Commonwealth	140	Riga Cathedral at Riga, Latvia	Europe
3 Papal States, early modern period	137	St Peter's Basilica at Vatican City, Italy	Europe
4 Holy Roman Empire	132	St Michaelis Church at Hamburg, Germany	Europe
=5 Holy Roman Empire	130	St Martin's Church at Landshut, Germany	Europe
=5 Holy Roman Empire	130	St Elizabeth's Church, Wroclaw, Poland	Europe
7 Holy Roman Empire	124	Cathedral of Our Lady at Antwerp, Belgium	Europe
=8 Swedish Empire	123	St Olaf's Church at Tallinn, Estonia	Europe
=8 Polish–Lithuanian Commonwealth	123	St Peter's Church at Riga, Latvia	Europe
10 Russian Empire	122	Peter and Paul Cathedral at St Petersburg, Russia	Europe

10 tallest buildings in the entire preindustrial era

Maximum approximate height reached by tallest portion of monumental building

Society	Approx. extent (area m²)	Building	Region	Period
1 Kingdom of England	159	Lincoln Cathedral at Lincoln, England	Europe	Medieval
2 Capetian kingdom	153	St Pierre's Cathedral at Beauvais, France	Europe	Early Modern
3 Principality of Rügen	151	St Mary's Church at Stralsund, Germany	Europe	Medieval
4 Kingdom of England	150	Old St Paul's Cathedral at London, England	Europe	Medieval

5 Teutonic Order	143,000	Malbork Castle at Malbork, Poland	Europe
6 Holy Roman Empire	70,000	Prague Castle at Prague, Czech Republic	Europe
7 Abbasid caliphate	39,000	Great Mosque at Samarra, Iraq	Southwest Asia
8 Medang kingdom	15,000–18,000	Borobudur Temple near Muntilan, Indonesia	Southeast Asia
9 Fatimid caliphate	14,000	Mosque of al-Hakim at Cairo, Egypt	North Africa
10 Capetian kingdom	10,000	Cathédrale Notre-Dame at Amiens, France	Europe

10 largest buildings by total area: early modern

Total approximate area encompassed by monumental building

Society	Approx. extent (area m²)	Building	Region
1 Mughal Empire	170,000	Taj Mahal at Agra, India	South Asia
2 Qing dynasty	160,000	Gardens of Perfect Brightness, aka Old Summer Palace at Beijing, China	East Asia
3 Ming dynasty	150,000	Forbidden City at Beijing, China	East Asia
4 Inca Empire	130,000	Sacsayhuamán Citadel at Cusco, Peru	South America
5 Bourbon kingdom	67,000	Palace of Versailles at Versailles, France	Europe
6 Ottoman Empire	45,000	Dolmabahçe Palace at Istanbul, Turkey	West Asia
7 Spanish Habsburg Empire	30,000	El Escorial at San Lorenzo de El Escorial, Spain	Europe
=8 Papal States, early modern period	33,000	St Peter's Basilica at Vatican City, Italy	Europe
=8 Tokugawa Shogunate	33,000	Central Honmaru palace complex at Edo, Japan	East Asia
10 Valois kingdom	18,000	Château de Chambord at Chambord, France	Europe

10 largest buildings by total area in the entire preindustrial era

Total approximate area encompassed by monumental building

	Society	Approx. extent (area m²)	Building	Region	Period
1	Angkor kingdom	820,000	Angkor Wat at Angkor, Cambodia	Southeast Asia	Medieval
2	Tang dynasty	690,000	Eastern Palace of the Crown Prince at Taijigong Palace City, Chang'an	East Asia	Medieval
3	Asuka kingdom	640,000	Imperial Palace at Fujiwara, Japan	East Asia	Medieval
4	Imperial Qin	600,000	Epang Hall, Qin Epang Palace at Shaanxi, China	East Asia	Ancient
5	Wari Empire	470,000	Pikillacta complex at Pikillacta, Peru	South America	Medieval
6	Mughal Empire	170,000	Taj Mahal at Agra, India	South Asia	Early Modern
7	Qing dynasty	160,000	Gardens of Perfect Brightness; aka Old Summer Palace at Beijing, China	East Asia	Early Modern
=8	Kofun period Japan	150,000	Diasen Tumulus Burial Mound at Osaka, Japan	East Asia	Ancient
=8	Ming dynasty	150,000	Forbidden City at Beijing, China	East Asia	Early Modern
10	Teutonic Order	143,000	Malbork Castle at Malbork, Poland	Europe	Medieval

10 tallest buildings: ancient

Maximum approximate height reached by tallest portion of monumental building

	Society	Approx. height (m)	Building	Region
1	Old Kingdom Egypt	147	Great Pyramid at Giza, Egypt	North Africa
2	Ptolemaic kingdom	130	Lighthouse at Alexandria, Egypt	North Africa
3	Kingdom of Anuradhapura	122	Jetavanaramaya Stupa at Anuradhapura, Sri Lanka	South Asia
4	Old Kingdom Egypt	105	Red Pyramid at Dahshur, Egypt	North Africa
5	Kingdom of Ruhuna	90–100	Ruwanwelisaya Stupa at Anuradhapura, Sri Lanka	South Asia
6	Old Kingdom Egypt	93	Meidum Pyramid at El Wasta, Egypt	North Africa
7	Mayan Empire	72	La Danta Temple (300 BCE) at El Petén, Guatemala	Central America
8	Old Kingdom Egypt	62	Step Pyramid at Saqqara, Egypt	North Africa
9	Phrygian kingdom	60	Burial Mound (megaron) at Gordion, Turkey	Europe
10	Greco-Bactrian kingdom	50	Theatre at Ai-Khanoum, Afghanistan	Central Asia

10 tallest buildings: medieval

Maximum approximate height reached by tallest portion of monumental building

	Society	Approx. height (m)	Building	Region
1	Kingdom of England	159	Lincoln Cathedral at Lincoln, England	Europe
2	Principality of Rügen	151	St Mary's Church at Stralsund, Germany	Europe
3	Kingdom of England	150	Old St Paul's Cathedral at London, England	Europe
4	Valois kingdom	142	Strasbourg Cathedral at Strasbourg, France	Europe
=5	Northern Wei dynasty	136	Yongning Pagoda at Luoyang, China	East Asia
=5	Habsburg dynasty	136	St Stephen's Cathedral at Vienna, Austria	Europe
7	Holy Roman Empire	134	St Lambert's Cathedral at Liège, Belgium	Europe
8	Holy Roman Empire	132	St Nicolas Church at Rostock, Germany	Europe
9	Kingdom of England	131	Malmesbury Abbey at Malmesbury, England	Europe
10	Holy Roman Empire	125	St Mary's Church at Lübeck, Germany	Europe

5 Old Kingdom Egypt	147	Great Pyramid at Giza, Egypt	North Africa	Ancient
6 Valois kingdom	142	Strasbourg Cathedral at Strasbourg, France	Europe	Medieval
7 Polish–Lithuanian Commonwealth	140	Riga Cathedral at Riga, Latvia	Europe	Early Modern
8 Papal States	137	St Peter's Basilica at Vatican City, Italy	Europe	Early Modern
=9 Northern Wei dynasty	136	Yongning Pagoda at Luoyang, China	East Asia	Medieval
=9 Habsburg dynasty	136	St Stephen's Cathedral at Vienna, Austria	Europe	Medieval

10 costliest monuments to build in the entire preindustrial era

Total approximate number of combined labour-years required to complete monumental building*

Society	Approx. labour-years	Building/Region		Period
1 Qin Empire	9m	Great Wall, northern China	East Asia	Ancient
2 Angkor kingdom	2.56m	Angkor Wat at Angkor, Cambodia	Southeast Asia	Medieval
3 Ming dynasty	1.5m	Forbidden City at Beijing, China	East Asia	Medieval
4 Old Kingdom Egypt	400,000	Great Pyramid at Giza, Egypt	North Africa	Ancient
5 Roman Principate	96,000	Colosseum at Rome, Italy	Europe	Ancient
6 Capetian kingdom	20,000	Cathédrale Notre-Dame at Amiens, France	Europe	Medieval
7 Medang kingdom	10,000–22,500	Borobudur Temple at Muntilan, Indonesia	Southeast Asia	Medieval
8 Wari Empire	15,800	Pikillacta complex at Pikillacta, Peru	South America	Medieval
9 China, Erligang culture	15,300	Zhengzhou wall at Zhengzhou, China	East Asia	Ancient
10 China, Longshan culture	3,300	Walls at Taosi, China	East Asia	Ancient

* *Labour-years calculated as number of people working on the monument per year multiplied by number of years it took to construct.*

10 largest fielded armies: ancient

Total approximate size of the largest army that fought in any specific battle

	Society	Approx. army size	Region
1	Achaemenid Persian Empire	340,000	Southwest Asia
=2	Western Jin dynasty	200,000–300,000	East Asia
=2	Qin Empire	200,000–300,000	East Asia
4	Eastern Han Empire	220,000–240,000	East Asia
5	Roman Principate	175,000–200,000	Europe
6	Eastern Roman Empire	110,000	Europe/West Asia
=7	Wei State, Warring States period	100,000	East Asia
=7	Western Han	100,000	East Asia
=7	Late Roman Republic	100,000	Europe
=7	Roman Dominate	100,000	Europe

10 largest fielded armies: medieval

Total approximate size of the largest army that fought in any specific battle

	Society	Approx. army size	Region
1	Sui dynasty	1m	East Asia
2	Tang dynasty	200,000–450,000	East Asia
3	Mongolian Empire	240,000	Central Asia
4	Mamluk sultanate	200,000	West Asia
5	Timurid Empire	140,000–200,000	Central Asia
=6	Umayyad caliphate	135,000	Southwest Asia
=6	Abbasid caliphate	135,000	Southwest Asia
8	Ghurid dynasty	120,000	Southwest Asia
9	Inca Empire	100,000	South America
10	Seljuq sultanate	80,000–100,000	West Asia

10 largest fielded armies: early modern

Total approximate size of the largest army that fought in any specific battle

	Society	Approx. army size	Region
1	Bourbon kingdom	300,000–350,000	Europe
2	Qing dynasty	340,500	East Asia
3	Tsardom of Russia	260,000	Europe
4	Ottoman Empire	200,000	West Asia
5	Azuchi–Momoyama period Japan	168,000	East Asia
6	Habsburg Spanish Empire	150,000	Europe
7	Mughal Empire	130,000	South Asia
8	Tokugawa Shogunate	125,000	East Asia
9	Rattanakosin kingdom	100,000	Southeast Asia
10	Ayutthaya kingdom	80,000	Southeast Asia

10 largest fielded armies in the entire preindustrial era

Total approximate size of the largest army that fought in any specific battle

	Society	Approx. army size	Region	Period
1	Sui dynasty	1m	East Asia	Medieval
2	Tang dynasty	200,000–450,000	East Asia	Medieval
3	Bourbon kingdom	300,000–350,000	Europe	Early Modern
4	Qing dynasty	340,500	East Asia	Early Modern
5	Achaemenid Persian Empire	340,000	Southwest Asia	Ancient
=6	Western Jin dynasty	200,000–300,000	East Asia	Ancient
=6	Qin Empire	200,000–300,000	East Asia	Ancient
8	Tsardom of Russia	260,000	Europe	Early Modern
9	Eastern Han Empire	220,000–240,000	East Asia	Ancient
10	Ottoman Empire	200,000	West Asia	Early Modern

10 longest fortification walls in the entire preindustrial era

Total approximate length of a permanent fortification structure built to protect a large territory

	Society	Approx. length (km)	Region	Period
1	Ming dynasty	6,700–8,800	East Asia	Early Modern
2	Western Han Empire	7,200	East Asia	Medieval
3	Qin Empire	3,000	East Asia	Ancient
4	Later Jin dynasty	1,700	East Asia	Medieval
5	Kievan Rus kingdom	900–1,000	Europe	Medieval
6	Mi-nyak Tangut kingdom	800	East Asia	Medieval
7	Khitan Empire	750	Central Asia	Medieval
8	Roman Principate	568	Europe	Ancient
9	Goguryeo kingdom	500	East Asia	Medieval
10	Ur – dynasty III	190–300	Southwest Asia	Ancient

10 bloodiest human sacrifices in the entire preindustrial era

Total approximate number of victims of a single human sacrifice ritual*

	Society	Approx. no. victims	Region	Period	Sacrifice event
1	Aztec Empire	2,000–4,000	North America	Medieval	Re-consecration of the temple atTenochtitlan
=2	China, Erligang culture	340	East Asia	Ancient	Victims buried at Xibeigang royal tombs
=2	Early Dynastic Egypt	340	North Africa	Ancient	Sacrificial attendants at Abydos royal tombs
4	Shang dynasty	160–180	East Asia	Ancient	Sacrificial attendants in elite burial tombs
5	Khitan Empire	100–200	Central Asia	Medieval	Sacrificial attendants in elite burials
6	Chimu Empire	140	South America	Medieval	Mass sacrifice of children
7	Ashanti kingdom	70	Sub-Saharan Africa	Early Modern	Sacrifice of war captives
8	Mississippi Valley, Cahokia settlement	50	North America	Medieval	Ritual sacrifice of female victims

9	Second Dynasty Egypt	6–15	North Africa	Ancient	Sacrificial attendants at tomb of Pharaoh Khasekhemwy
10	China, Longshan culture	6–8	East Asia	Ancient	Victims buried in construction pits at monumental buildings

* *Human sacrifice defined as deliberate and ritualised killing of an individual to please or placate supernatural beings.*

10 most widely attended collective rituals: ancient

Total approximate number of participants at a single collective ritual held as part of a society's official cult and/or ruling ideology*

	Society	Approx. no. attendants	Region	Ritual
=1	Roman Empire	250,000–350,000	Europe	Spectators of chariot races at Circus Maximus, Rome
=1	Roman Republic	250,000–350,000	Europe	Spectators of chariot races at Circus Maximus, Rome
=1	Ostrogothic kingdom	250,000–350,000	Europe	Spectators of chariot races at Circus Maximus, Rome
4	Ptolemaic kingdom	100,000	North Africa	Ptolemaieia festival at Alexandria
5	Eastern Roman Empire	60,000	West Asia	Spectators of chariot races at Hippodrome, Constantinople
6	Kingdom of Yehuda	10,000– 48,000	West Asia	Pilgrimage to Temple at Jerusalem
7	Minoan Crete	12,000–30,000	Europe	Bull leaping ritual
8	Saite period Egypt	11,000	North Africa	Opet festival procession at Thebes
9	Greco-Bactrian kingdom	5,000	Central Asia	Civic festival at Epidauros
10	Monte Albán period	2,000–5,000	North America	Public sacrifice rituals at Main Plaza, Monte Albán

* *Collective ritual defined as any ritual in which two or more people participate, excluding private rituals (such as treatments and therapies).*

10 most widely attended collective rituals: medieval

Total approximate number of participants at a single collective ritual held as part of a society's official cult and/or ruling ideology*

Society	Approx. no. attendants	Region	Ritual
1 Yuan dynasty	75–85m	East Asia	Birthday celebration for Great Khan, Dadu
2 Papal States, medieval period	200,000	Europe	Jubilee, Rome
=3 Capetian kingdom	110,000–228,000	Europe	Royal procession, Paris
=3 Valois kingdom	110,000–228,000	Europe	Royal procession, Paris
5 Byzantine Empire	60,000	West Asia	Spectators of chariot races at Hippodrome, Constantinople
6 Northern Song dynasty	22,000	East Asia	Palace exams, Kaifeng
7 Wagadu kingdom	20,000	West Africa	Royal funeral
8 Mongolian Empire	5,000	East Asia	Great Quriltai ceremony, Karakorum
9 Cahokia, Lohmann-Stirling period	2,400–21,000	North America	Communal feasting, Cahokia
10 Early Angkor kingdom	2,000–4,000	Southeast Asia	Oath of allegiance to Sūryavarman I, Angkor

* Collective ritual defined as any ritual in which two or more people participate, excluding private rituals (such as treatments and therapies).

10 most widely attended collective rituals: early modern

Total approximate number of participants at a single collective ritual held as part of a society's official cult and/or ruling ideology*

Society	Approx. no. attendants	Region	Ritual
1 Ashanti Empire	2m	West Africa	Apo festival, Techiman
2 Garo Hills, colonial period	250,000	South Asia	Pilgrimage for Kumbh Mela ceremony, Haridwar
3 Bourbon kingdom	110,000–228,000	Europe	Royal procession, Paris
4 Rattanakosin kingdom	25,000	Southeast Asia	Royal Kathina, Ayutthaya
5 Ayutthaya kingdom	22,500	Southeast Asia	Royal Kathina, Ayutthaya
6 Ashanti Empire	17,000	West Africa	Yam festival

7	Garo Hills, colonial period	7,600	South Asia	Asongtata ceremony
8	Garo Hills, colonial period	5,600	South Asia	Denbilsia festival
9	Sakha peoples, Russia	3,600	Europe	Ayy ysyaxa Spring Festival
10	Iban peoples, Borneo	1,400	Southeast Asia	Rites of Manggol agriculture festival

* *Collective ritual defined as any ritual in which two or more people participate, excluding private rituals (such as treatments and therapies).*

10 most widely attended collective rituals in the entire preindustrial era

Total approximate number of participants at a single collective ritual held as part of a society's official cult and/or ruling ideology*

	Society	Approx. no. attendants	Region	Period	Ritual
1	Yuan dynasty	75–85m	East Asia	Medieval	Birthday celebration for Great Khan, Dadu
2	Ashanti Empire	2m	West Africa	Early Modern	Apo festival, Techiman
=3	Roman Principate	250,000–350,000	Europe	Ancient	Spectators of chariot races at Circus Maximus, Rome
=3	Roman Republic	250,000–350,000	Europe	Ancient	Spectators of chariot races at Circus Maximus, Rome
=3	Ostrogothic kingdom	250,000–350,000	Europe		Spectators of chariot races at Circus Maximus, Rome
6	India, colonial period	250,000	South Asia	Early Modern	Pilgrimage for Kumbh Mela ceremony, Haridwar
=7	Bourbon kingdom	110,000–228,000	Europe	Early Modern	Royal procession, Paris
=7	Capetian kingdom	110,000–228,000	Europe	Medieval	Royal procession, Paris
=7	Lombard kingdom	110,000–228,000	Europe	Medieval	Royal procession, Paris
10	Papal States, medieval period	200,000	Europe	Medieval	Jubilee, Rome

* *Collective ritual defined as any ritual in which two or more people participate, excluding private rituals (such as treatments and therapies).*

Mali: Mali Empire

In the early 13th century, several Malinke chiefdoms from the upper Niger Delta region united against the Sosso kingdom, forming the Mali Empire, the largest of the medieval West African empires. Under Musa I ("Mansa Musa") the Mali Empire controlled over 24 cities and their surrounding territories, bounded by the Atlantic, the Niger Inland Delta, the Sahara and the tropical forest belt. Mansa Musa is famed for his patronage of Islam and his lavish distribution of gold while on pilgrimage to Mecca in 1325 CE. The cities of Mali were cosmopolitan, exporting gold, ivory, salt and enslaved people across the Sahara. Their characteristic mud-brick architecture, known as *banco*, can still be admired today.

General
Duration 1230–1410 CE
Languages Mande (Afro-Asiatic), Arabic (Afro-Asiatic)
Preceded by Sosso kingdom
Succeeded by Mande states

Territory
Total area (km²) >1.5m

People
Population 4–5m
Largest city 12,000–17,000 (based on evidence that medium-sized towns had 10,000–15,000 inhabitants).
Standing army 8,700 (size of King Mansa Musa's military escort in his famed pilgrimage to Mecca).

Social scale

Settlement hierarchy 1. Capital; 2. Market towns; 3. Mud-walled towns (*kafu*); 4. Villages.

Administrative hierarchy 1. King; 2. Court administrators; 3. Regional governors; 4. Village headmen.

Institutions

Legal code Mixed. Customary law prevailed but significant Muslim minority followed Islamic law.

Bureaucracy Limited. Court administrators known to have existed but very little else known about them.

Religious validation of rule Unclear 1230–1310 CE; divine support after Islamic conversion 1311–1410.

Property rights Unclear. Cultural understanding that anyone could have their own patch of land; sale of land not common practice.

Price controls No data

Banking regulations Probably present

Economy

Taxation Taxes on land, trade and production.

Coinage Unclear. Evidence of local manufacture of unstamped gold disks (*sola*).

Credit Loans were issued and debts were acknowledged in writing.

Agricultural practices

Main crop Rice

Irrigation Absent

Fertilising Absent

Cropping system A mixture of short-fallow and shifting cultivation

Metallurgy

Base metals Bronze, iron and perhaps steel

Military equipment

Handheld weapons Swords, spears and lances

Armour Mail coats, breastplates, shields, helmets and limb protection; largely reserved for nobles.

Projectiles Javelins and simple bows

Incendiaries No evidence

Long walls No long walls known to have been built.

Well-being

Life expectancy No data

Average adult stature No data

Irrigation & drinking water Probably present

Health care No data

Alimentary support No data

Famine relief No data

(In)equalities

Social mobility Probably absent

Occupational mobility Probably absent

Gender equality Unclear, but worth noting that the Manden or Kurukan Fuga Charter, a sort of oral "constitution" for the Mali Empire, gave equal rights to men and women.

Slavery Probably present. Chattel slavery; war captives usually enslaved.

Human sacrifice Probably absent. No clear evidence that it was practised; as Islamic beliefs spread, they would have included prohibition against human sacrifice.

Religion

Majority religious practices Mali religion; Sufi Islam

Egypt: Mamluk sultanate

The Mamluks wrested power from the Ayyubid caliphate, taking control over much of the Levant along with Egypt and parts of the Arab peninsula. Mamluk is an Arabic term used to designate the class of highly trained enslaved people mobilised by medieval Islamic rulers for military and administrative duties. The Mamluks oversaw an era of prosperity in Egypt, which peaked under the reign of Sultan Nasiri. However, prosperity was brought to an end by the Black Death, which arrived in Alexandria in 1347 CE. Mamluk law prevented the children of mamluks from becoming mamluks – a means of thwarting nepotism and corruption. Consequently, the ruling elite had to be constantly replaced by new "slave" recruits taken mainly from Crimea and the Caucasus.

General
Duration 1260–1517 CE
Language Arabic (Afro-Asiatic)
Preceded by Ayyubid sultanate
Succeeded by Ottoman Empire

Territory
Total area (km²) 2.1m

People
Population 6–7m in 1300 CE; 4.8m in 1400; 6m in 1500
Largest city 200,000 in 1300 CE; 150,000–350,000 in 1400;
　　　150,000–400,000 in 1500 (Cairo).
Standing army 40,000–50,000

5	Teutonic Order	143,000	Malbork Castle at Malbork, Poland	Europe
6	Holy Roman Empire	70,000	Prague Castle at Prague, Czech Republic	Europe
7	Abbasid caliphate	39,000	Great Mosque at Samarra, Iraq	Southwest Asia
8	Medang kingdom	15,000–18,000	Borobudur Temple near Muntilan, Indonesia	Southeast Asia
9	Fatimid caliphate	14,000	Mosque of al-Hakim at Cairo, Egypt	North Africa
10	Capetian kingdom	10,000	Cathédrale Notre-Dame at Amiens, France	Europe

10 largest buildings by total area: early modern

Total approximate area encompassed by monumental building

Society	Approx. extent (area m²)	Building	Region
1 Mughal Empire	170,000	Taj Mahal at Agra, India	South Asia
2 Qing dynasty	160,000	Gardens of Perfect Brightness; aka Old Summer Palace at Beijing, China	East Asia
3 Ming dynasty	150,000	Forbidden City at Beijing, China	East Asia
4 Inca Empire	130,000	Sacsayhuamán Citadel at Cusco, Peru	South America
5 Bourbon kingdom	67,000	Palace of Versailles at Versailles, France	Europe
6 Ottoman Empire	45,000	Dolmabahçe Palace at Istanbul, Turkey	West Asia
7 Spanish Habsburg Empire	30,000	El Escorial at San Lorenzo de El Escorial, Spain	Europe
=8 Papal States, early modern period	33,000	St Peter's Basilica at Vatican City, Italy	Europe
=8 Tokugawa Shogunate	33,000	Central Honmaru palace complex at Edo, Japan	East Asia
10 Valois kingdom	18,000	Château de Chambord at Chambord, France	Europe

10 largest buildings by total area in the entire preindustrial era

Total approximate area encompassed by monumental building

	Society	Approx. extent (area m²)	Building	Region	Period
1	Angkor kingdom	820,000	Angkor Wat at Angkor, Cambodia	Southeast Asia	Medieval
2	Tang dynasty	690,000	Eastern Palace of the Crown Prince at Taijigong Palace City, Chang'an	East Asia	Medieval
3	Asuka kingdom	640,000	Imperial Palace at Fujiwara, Japan	East Asia	Medieval
4	Imperial Qin	600,000	Epang Hall, Qin Epang Palace at Shaanxi, China	East Asia	Ancient
5	Wari Empire	470,000	Pikillacta complex at Pikillacta, Peru	South America	Medieval
6	Mughal Empire	170,000	Taj Mahal at Agra, India	South Asia	Early Modern
7	Qing dynasty	160,000	Gardens of Perfect Brightness; aka Old Summer Palace at Beijing, China	East Asia	Early Modern
=8	Kofun period Japan	150,000	Diasen Tumulus Burial Mound at Osaka, Japan	East Asia	Ancient
=8	Ming dynasty	150,000	Forbidden City at Beijing, China	East Asia	Early Modern
10	Teutonic Order	143,000	Malbork Castle at Malbork, Poland	Europe	Medieval

10 tallest buildings: ancient

Maximum approximate height reached by tallest portion of monumental building

	Society	Approx. height (m)	Building	Region
1	Old Kingdom Egypt	147	Great Pyramid at Giza, Egypt	North Africa
2	Ptolemaic kingdom	130	Lighthouse at Alexandria, Egypt	North Africa
3	Kingdom of Anuradhapura	122	Jetavanaramaya Stupa at Anuradhapura, Sri Lanka	South Asia

4 Old Kingdom Egypt	105	Red Pyramid at Dahshur, Egypt	North Africa
5 Kingdom of Ruhuna	90–100	Ruwanwelisaya Stupa at Anuradhapura, Sri Lanka	South Asia
6 Old Kingdom Egypt	93	Meidum Pyramid at El Wasta, Egypt	North Africa
7 Mayan Empire	72	La Danta Temple (300 BCE) at El Petén, Guatemala	Central America
8 Old Kingdom Egypt	62	Step Pyramid at Saqqara, Egypt	North Africa
9 Phrygian kingdom	60	Burial Mound (megaron) at Gordion, Turkey	Europe
10 Greco-Bactrian kingdom	50	Theatre at Ai-Khanoum, Afghanistan	Central Asia

10 tallest buildings: medieval

Maximum approximate height reached by tallest portion of monumental building

Society	Approx. height (m)	Building	Region
1 Kingdom of England	159	Lincoln Cathedral at Lincoln, England	Europe
2 Principality of Rügen	151	St Mary's Church at Stralsund, Germany	Europe
3 Kingdom of England	150	Old St Paul's Cathedral at London, England	Europe
4 Valois kingdom	142	Strasbourg Cathedral at Strasbourg, France	Europe
=5 Northern Wei dynasty	136	Yongning Pagoda at Luoyang, China	East Asia
=5 Habsburg dynasty	136	St Stephen's Cathedral at Vienna, Austria	Europe
7 Holy Roman Empire	134	St Lambert's Cathedral at Liège, Belgium	Europe
8 Holy Roman Empire	132	St Nicolas Church at Rostock, Germany	Europe
9 Kingdom of England	131	Malmesbury Abbey at Malmesbury, England	Europe
10 Holy Roman Empire	125	St Mary's Church at Lübeck, Germany	Europe

10 tallest buildings: early modern

Maximum approximate height reached by tallest portion of monumental building

Society	Approx. height (m)	Building	Region
1 Capetian kingdom	153	St Pierre's Cathedral at Beauvais, France	Europe
2 Polish–Lithuanian Commonwealth	140	Riga Cathedral at Riga, Latvia	Europe
3 Papal States, early modern period	137	St Peter's Basilica at Vatican City, Italy	Europe
4 Holy Roman Empire	132	St Michaelis Church at Hamburg, Germany	Europe
=5 Holy Roman Empire	130	St Martin's Church at Landshut, Germany	Europe
=5 Holy Roman Empire	130	St Elizabeth's Church, Wroclaw, Poland	Europe
7 Holy Roman Empire	124	Cathedral of Our Lady at Antwerp, Belgium	Europe
=8 Swedish Empire	123	St Olaf's Church at Tallinn, Estonia	Europe
=8 Polish–Lithuanian Commonwealth	123	St Peter's Church at Riga, Latvia	Europe
10 Russian Empire	122	Peter and Paul Cathedral at St Petersburg, Russia	Europe

10 tallest buildings in the entire preindustrial era

Maximum approximate height reached by tallest portion of monumental building

Society	Approx. extent (area m²)	Building	Region	Period
1 Kingdom of England	159	Lincoln Cathedral at Lincoln, England	Europe	Medieval
2 Capetian kingdom	153	St Pierre's Cathedral at Beauvais, France	Europe	Early Modern
3 Principality of Rügen	151	St Mary's Church at Stralsund, Germany	Europe	Medieval
4 Kingdom of England	150	Old St Paul's Cathedral at London, England	Europe	Medieval

Adoption of bureaucracy by world region

(Refers to the adoption of full-time administrative specialists)

Society	Region	Approx. time of adoption
Bronze Age Susa	Southwest Asia	early 4th millennium BCE
Pre-dynastic Egypt	North Africa	mid-4th millennium BCE
Indus Valley, urban period	South Asia	late 3rd millennium BCE
Minoan Crete	Europe	early 2nd millennium BCE
Shang dynasty	East Asia	late 2nd millennium BCE
Baiyue kingdoms	Southeast Asia	4th century BCE
Kangju Federation	Central Asia	2nd century BCE
Teotihuacan	North America	3rd century CE
Peru, late intermediate period	South America	13th century CE
Ashanti Empire	Sub-Saharan Africa	18th century CE
Colonial period Papua New Guinea, Orokaiva peoples	Oceania	18th century CE

Adoption of state postal service by world region

(Refers to the adoption of dedicated communications infrastructure)

Society	Region	Approx. time of adoption
Achaemenid Empire	Southwest Asia	6th century BCE
Qin Empire	East Asia	4th century BCE
Mauryan Empire	South Asia	4th century BCE
Ptolemaic kingdom	North Africa	3rd century BCE
Roman Principate	Europe	1st century BCE
Mongolian Empire	Central Asia	13th century CE
Peru, Spanish colonial period	South America	16th century CE
Ayutthaya kingdom	Southeast Asia	16th century CE
Mississippi Valley, French colonial period	North America	17th century CE
Innovation remained absent until modern period or evidence is unavailable for these regions	*Sub-Saharan Africa Oceania*	

Adoption of a formalised law code by world region

(Refers to the adoption of a formal code of rules/procedures, usually but not always written)

Society	Region	Approx. time of adoption
Ur Kingdom dynasty III	Southwest Asia	late 3rd millennium BCE
Old Kingdom Egypt	North Africa	early 2nd millennium BCE
Minoan Crete	Europe	8th century BCE
State of Chu	East Asia	5th century BCE
Mauryan Empire	South Asia	4th century BCE
Greco-Bactrian kingdom	Central Asia	3rd century BCE
Funan kingdom	Southeast Asia	3rd century CE
Wagadu kingdom of Ghana	Sub-Saharan Africa	11th century CE
Killke period Inca	South America	13th century CE
Aztec Empire	North America	15th century CE
Kingdom of Hawaii, post-Kamehameha period	Oceania	19th century CE

Adoption of calendars by world region

(Refers to the adoption of a formalised written system for marking time/seasons)

Society	Region	Approx. time of adoption
Early Bronze Age Susa	Southwest Asia	early 4th millennium BCE
Early Dynastic Egypt	North Africa	late 4th millennium BCE
China, Erlitou culture	East Asia	early 2nd millennium BCE
Minoan Crete	Europe	mid-2nd millennium BCE
Basin of Mexico, late classic period	North America	6th century BCE
Mauryan Empire	South Asia	4th century BCE
Baiyue kingdoms	Southeast Asia	3rd century BCE
Greco-Bactrian kingdom	Central Asia	3rd century BCE
Wagadu kingdom of Ghana	Sub-Saharan Africa	11th century CE
Peru, Spanish colonial period	South America	16th century CE
Innovation remained absent until modern period or evidence is unavailable for this region	*Oceania*	

Adoption of scientific literature by world region

(Refers to the adoption of writing concerning mathematics, natural sciences or social sciences)

Society	Region	Approx. time of adoption
Early Bronze Age Susa	Southwest Asia	early 4th millennium BCE
Early Dynastic Egypt	North Africa	late 4th millennium BCE
Western Zhou dynasty	East Asia	late 2nd millennium BCE
Roman Republic	Europe	6th century BCE
Mauryan Empire	South Asia	4th century BCE
Baiyue kingdoms	Southeast Asia	3rd century BCE
Greco-Bactrian kingdom	Central Asia	3rd century BCE
Mayan period Mesoamerica	North America	8th century CE
Songhai Empire	Sub-Saharan Africa	16th century CE
Kingdom of Hawaii, post-Kamehameha period	Oceania	19th century CE
Innovation remained absent until modern period or evidence is unavailable for this region	*South America*	

Adoption of fiction writing by world region

(Refers to the adoption of written fiction literature, including prose)

Society	Region	Approx. time of adoption
Old Kingdom Egypt	North Africa	mid-3rd millennium BCE
Akkadian Empire	Southwest Asia	late 3rd millennium BCE
Western Zhou dynasty	East Asia	late 2nd millennium BCE
Roman Republic	Europe	6th century BCE
Mauryan Empire	South Asia	4th century BCE
Baiyue kingdoms	Southeast Asia	3rd century BCE
Greco-Bactrian kingdom	Central Asia	3rd century BCE
Wagadu kingdom of Ghana	Sub-Saharan Africa	11th century CE
Peru, Spanish colonial period	South America	16th century CE
Mississippi Valley, French colonial period	North America	17th century CE
Innovation remained absent until modern period or evidence is unavailable for this region	*Oceania*	

Adoption of monogamy by world region

(Refers to the adoption of monogamy as widely practised, either by law or custom)

Society	Region	Approx. time of adoption
Ur Kingdom city-state III	Southwest Asia	late 3rd millennium BCE
New Kingdom Egypt	North Africa	mid-2nd millennium BCE
Oaxaca Valley, Rosario culture	North America	8th century BCE
Roman kingdom	Europe	8th century BCE
Ganga Valley, Mahajanapada era	South Asia	7th century BCE
Kalingga kingdom	Southeast Asia	6th century CE
Colombia, Tairona peoples	South America	11th century CE
Innovation remained absent until modern period or evidence is unavailable for these regions	*Central Asia East Asia Oceania Sub-Saharan Africa*	

Adoption of rule by god-kings by world region

(Refers to the adoption of the idea that rulers are living gods, either by formal declaration or widespread belief)

Society	Region	Approx. time of adoption
Naqada period Egypt	North Africa	mid-4th millennium BCE
Minoan Crete	Europe	early 2nd millennium BCE
Qin Empire	East Asia	4th century BCE
Seleucid kingdom	Southwest Asia	3rd century BCE
Greco-Bactrian kingdom	Central Asia	3rd century BCE
Satavahana Empire	South Asia	2nd century BCE
Kofun kingdom	East Asia	3rd century CE
Killke period Inca	South America	11th century CE
Innovation remained absent until modern period or evidence is unavailable for these regions	*North America Sub-Saharan Africa Oceania*	

Adoption of firearms by world region

(Refers to the adoption of hand-held gunpowder devices, such as muskets, pistols and rifles)

Society	Region	Approx. time of adoption
Yuan dynasty	East Asia	13th century CE
Valois kingdom	Europe	14th century CE
Ottoman Empire	Southwest Asia	15th century CE
Ottoman Empire	North Africa	15th century CE
Mamluk sultanate	North Africa	15th century CE
Delhi sultanate	South Asia	15th century CE
Mataram kingdom	Southeast Asia	16th century CE
Oneota Mississippi Valley peoples	North America	16th century CE
Spanish Empire	South America	16th century CE
Khanate of Bukhara	Central Asia	17th century CE
Ashanti kingdom	Sub-Saharan Africa	18th century CE
Kamehameha's kingdom Hawaii	Oceania	18th century CE

Adoption of paper currency by world region

(Refers to the adoption of paper money as legal tender)

Society	Region	Approx. time of adoption
Western Han Empire	East Asia	3rd century BCE
Delhi sultanate	South Asia	13th century CE
Ilkhanate	Central Asia	13th century CE
Papal States	Europe	17th century CE
Mississippi Valley, French colonial period	North America	18th century CE
Peru, Spanish colonial period	South America	18th century CE
Rattanakosin kingdom	Southeast Asia	19th century CE
Brooke Raj, colonial Borneo	Oceania	19th century CE
Ottoman Empire	Southwest Asia	19th century CE
Ottoman Empire	North Africa	19th century CE
Innovation remained absent until modern period or evidence is unavailable for this region	*Sub-Saharan Africa*	

Adoption of irrigation systems by world region

(Refers to the adoption and widespread use of any hydraulic infrastructure, such as large reservoirs, cisterns, canals and aqueducts)

Society	Region	Approx. time of adoption
Naqada period Egypt	North Africa	early 4th millennium BCE
Chalcolithic period Pakistan	South Asia	early 4th millennium BCE
Bronze Age Susa	Southwest Asia	early 4th millennium BCE
Sarazm peoples	Central Asia	mid-4th millennium BCE
France, Beaker culture	Europe	late 4th millennium BCE
Shang dynasty	East Asia	late 2nd millennium BCE
Baiyue kingdoms	Southeast Asia	4th century BCE
Peru, formative period culture	South America	3rd century CE
Oaxaca, Monte Albán period	North America	4th century CE
Jenné-jenno culture	Sub-Saharan Africa	5th century CE
Big Island Hawaii, pre-unification period	Oceania	13th century CE

Adoption of state-wide provision of drinking water by world region

(Refers to the adoption of publicly accessible sources of drinking water, such as public fountains, reservoirs and wells)

Society	Region	Approx. time of adoption
Indus Valley, urban period	South Asia	mid-3rd millennium BCE
Bronze Age Canaanite city-states	Southwest Asia	late 3rd millennium BCE
Iron Age Crete	Europe	early 1st millennium BCE
Achaemenid Empire	Central Asia	6th century BCE
Wei State, Warring States period	East Asia	5th century BCE
Egypt, inter-occupation period	North Africa	5th century BCE
Oaxaca, Monte Albán period	North America	4th century BCE
Funan kingdom	Southeast Asia	3rd century CE
Wari Empire	South America	7th century CE
Hawaiian kingdom	Oceania	19th century CE
Innovation remained absent until modern period or evidence is unavailable for this region	*Sub-Saharan Africa*	

Adoption of public markets by world region

(Refers to the adoption of publicly accessible open spaces for commerce, congregation and information exchange)

Society	Region	Approx. time of adoption
Old Kingdom Egypt	North Africa	3rd millennium BCE
Awan dynasty Elam	Southwest Asia	3rd millennium BCE
Minoan Crete	Europe	2nd millennium BCE
Kingdom of Wu, Warring States period	East Asia	8th century BCE
Achaemenid Empire	Central Asia	6th century BCE
Indo-Greek kingdom	South Asia	2nd century BCE
Jenné-jenno culture	Sub-Saharan Africa	5th century CE
Angkor kingdom	Southeast Asia	9th century CE
Tairona cultures, Colombia	South America	11th century CE
Mississippi Valley, French colonial period	North America	17th century CE
Papua New Guinea, British colonial period	Oceania	19th century CE

Adoption of state-run libraries by world region

(Refers to the adoption of publicly built infrastructure for holding and disseminating knowledge)

Society	Region	Approx. time of adoption
Early Dynastic Egypt	North Africa	early 3rd millennium BCE
Shang dynasty	East Asia	late 2nd millennium BCE
Neo-Assyrian Empire	Southwest Asia	early 1st millennium BCE
Roman kingdom	Europe	8th century BCE
Seleucid Empire	Central Asia	3rd century BCE
Kushan Empire	South Asia	1st century CE
Funan kingdom	Southeast Asia	3rd century CE
Jenné-jenno culture	Sub-Saharan Africa	13th century CE
Innovation remained absent until modern period or evidence is unavailable for these regions	*North America South America Oceania*	

Spread of agriculture, 10,000 BCE to 1880 CE

- 10,000–8000 BCE
- 8000–4000 BCE
- 4000 BCE to 1 CE
- 1–1880 CE

Spread of human sacrifice, 5000 BCE to 1880 CE

● 5000–2000 BCE   ● 2000–500 BCE   ● 500 BCE to 1000 CE   ● 1000–1880 CE

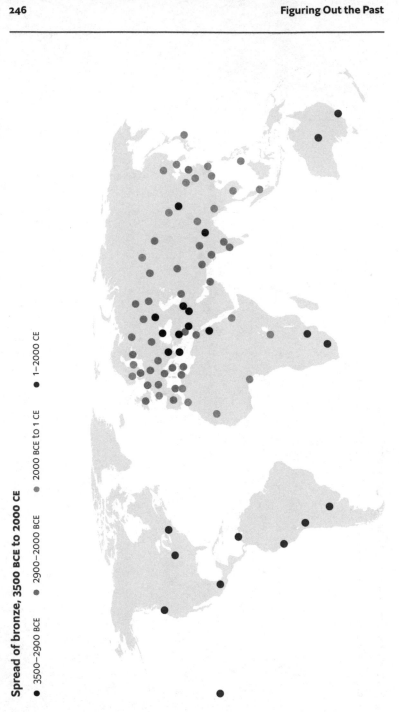

Spread of bronze, 3500 BCE to 2000 CE

● 3500–2900 BCE   ● 2900–2000 BCE   ● 2000 BCE to 1 CE   ● 1–2000 CE

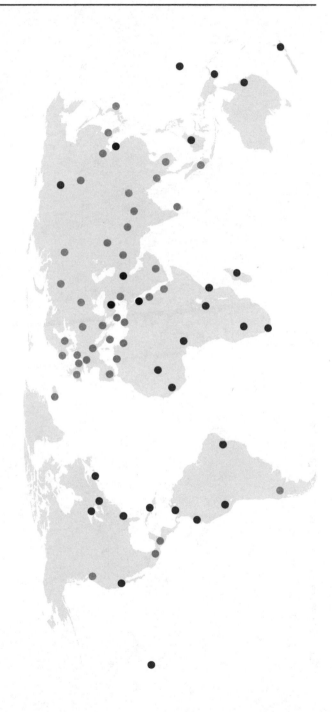

Spread of writing, 3200 BCE to 1920 CE

● 3200–2000 BCE   ● 2000 BCE to 1 CE   ● 1–1000 CE   ● 1000–1920

Spread of moralising religion, 2100 BCE to 1900 CE

● 2100–1000 BCE   ● 1000 BCE to 500 CE   ● 500–1250 CE   ● 1250–1900

Spread of chariots, 2000 BCE to 1780 CE

● 2000–1800 BCE ● 1800–1400 BCE ● 1400–1000 BCE ● 1000 BCE to 1780 CE

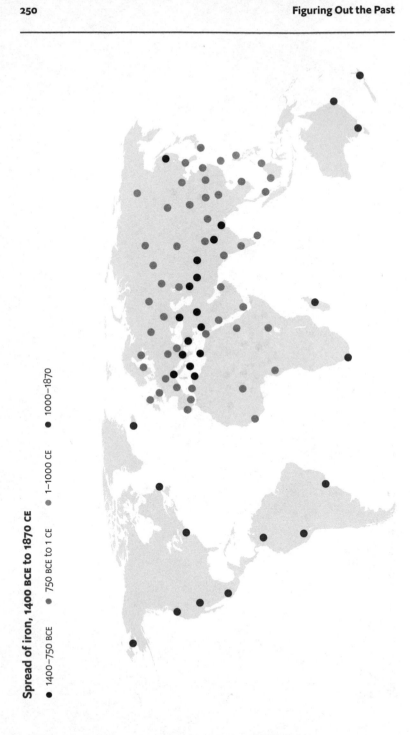

Spread of iron, 1400 BCE to 1870 CE

● 1400–750 BCE   ● 750 BCE to 1 CE   ● 1–1000 CE   ● 1000–1870

Spread of cavalry, 1000 BCE to 1870 CE

● 1000–700 BCE   ● 700 BCE to 1 CE   ● 1–700 CE   ● 700–1870

Spread of coinage, 600 BCE to 1900 CE

● 600–500 BCE　　● 500 BCE to 500 CE　　● 500–1250 CE　　● 1250–1900

Spread of gunpowder, 904–1945 CE

● 904–1000 CE   ● 1000–1300   ● 1300–1700   ● 1700–1945